m

m .17 MAR 2004

MANU...

Grammar of the Shot

media
MANUAL

Grammar of the Shot

Roy Thompson

Focal Press
OXFORD BOSTON JOHANNESBURG MELBOURNE NEW DELHI SINGAPORE

Focal Press
An imprint of Butterworth Heinemann
Linacre House, Jordan Hill, Oxford OX2 8DP
225 Wildwood Avenue, Woburn, MA 01801-2041
A division of Reed Educational and Professional Publishing Ltd

A member of the Reed Elsevier plc group

First published 1998

British Library Cataloguing in Publication Data
A catalogue record for this book is available from the British Library

Library of Congress Cataloguing in Publication Data
A catalogue record for this book is available from the Library of Congress

ISBN 0 240 51398 3

Typeset by Avocet Typeset, Brill, Aylesbury, Bucks
Printed and bound in Great Britain by Biddles Ltd of King's Lynn and
Guildford

Contents

Acknowledgements

It has been said that most books, somewhere in the foreword, contain an apology for what it is and an explanation of what it is not. If that is so, then this book will be no exception. It is not for experts, it is for beginners, students who are about to begin the long, arduous, depressing, boring, definitive precision craft which is still as exciting as it has always been.

It was Christian Grote, now retired from production, who first encouraged me to write down my ideas. During long hot evenings between shot and edit, in Kuala Lumpur, in Beijing and in Colombo we would while away the time arguing over the meaning of the very production words we had used that same day. It was the mutual exchange of ideas and ideals which gave me the incentive needed.

To Dietrich Berwanger, my thanks for making the wider issues understandable, and to his staff who showed me the never ending need for simplicity.

Also my thanks to Deutsche Welle for permission to use stills from programmes, Vinten for the use of some of their drawings and David Samuelson for permission to quote from his lens tables.

My sincere gratitude to Margaret Riley, who must be the most patient and understanding of all publishing editors. She understands that life in the business leaves little time for being an author.

With ordinary people most achievement is concerned with the enlargement of their own ego, mine is no different. So, I am conscious that if there is any success it is due mainly to those who taught me. The failures are mine alone. And if my ego has been lovingly kept within acceptable limits then there is only one person to thank, more than any other.

To K.T.

Introduction

People 'read' pictures as they do words, and pictures, like sentences, have their own grammar. Once that grammar is changed or omitted, either by design or ignorance, then many elements in the complex process of perception, of reading and understanding, are themselves changed.

We see things in a certain way, not by accident, but because we have learnt to 'read' the pictures. This learning process in some countries might be a formal visual education and in other countries it may be more haphazard. Nevertheless, the learning and reading process takes place. But just because we can read the picture does not mean we can understand it. In many art forms it is not a prerequisite that the artist must communicate, but Film and TV is made to be watched. Consequently it attempts to communicate by pictures and sounds.

What we try to say in pictures is often 'read' by the audience differently. To make pictures more understandable, picture makers have developed a series of 'visual clues', about size, shape, position, direction etc. These visual clues evolved when two-dimensional images began in the caves 12 000 years ago. Today, with electronic images, the 'visual clues' have become more subtle and the visual language more complex. But visual language still has a basic structure. It has its own principles, rules and conventions as does any other language.

Visual language has its own versions of full stops, its own versions of parentheses, of chapters and columns and margins, its own versions of tenses and syntax. It has a grammar. A picture maker must be able to use the grammar correctly, so that the visual story to be told will be clear and easily understood by all the audience.

When moving picture making began, the word 'shooter' was used to describe the person who worked the film camera. These days, 'cinematographer' better describes the more intricate work. In the early days of studio television, the engineers worked the camera and were called camera operators.

In Europe, the word 'man' was added to the word 'camera' and the new word became accepted by popular usage; 'videographer' was offered but was not retained. So, in referring to the job, the word 'cameraman' will be used, because it is the generic term. Popular usage decrees that 'Cameraman' means woman as much as it does man.

This manual is for those who are about to embark on a career in shooting pictures. It is for the novice. It concentrates purely on the 'classics' of shooting and has nothing to do with fashion or trend. It may be that 'classical shooting' is as dead as the dodo. Be that as it may, but when fashion pales and trend lies a dying, classical shooting will still go on. It must, because it is still the only way that we know to tell a story.

Roy Thompson, 1998

How do we see, what do we see?

There are two fundamentals to consider prior to any study of moving pictures. They are: What do we see? How do we see it?

There is a big difference between what an audience thinks it sees and what it actually sees. Moving picture makers have used this difference very sucessfully and over the years have refined it almost to a science. Moving picture makers have also taught the audience how to understand their pictures and have developed a visual (film) language which the audience has come to accept.

The two questions, therefore, 'What do I see?' and 'How do I see it?', refer to film language and hardly ever to reality. 'Reality!', said the Director, 'What's reality got to do with it? – I'm making a film!'

What do we see?

Moving pictures have *three* dimensions: width, height and depth. Imagine the three dimensions as a box. The first two of the dimensions are real but the third is created by illusion. Put another way, moving pictures have a frame around them, made up of width and height. Depth is the illusion, because 'in reality' a film or TV image is only an electronic or optical projection which has no thickness. The story we see takes place within the box, in the created depth and within the edges of the frame. If the subject of the story leaves the frame then extra boxes are needed to continue to tell the story. Also, in some instances, more detail needs to be seen, so the audience must move closer into the box. Each of the boxes or scenes are joined together, so that the audience does not notice how the scene has changed, only that it has.

This single audience requirement, to see what has happened but not to notice technically how it has happened, becomes the fundamental aim of the cameraman.

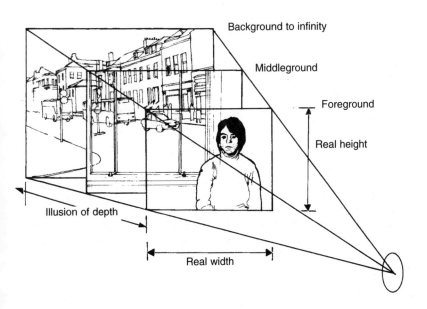

Background to infinity

Middleground

Foreground

Real height

Illusion of depth

Real width

The first two dimensions of the box, width and height, have changed in size many times since the early history. A story shown on an early screen would look absurd on today's screens and vice versa. There is an international agreement for the width and height of the frame for both TV and Film, but variations are still made. So the cameraman must first know which frame they are shooting within. Fortunately, even though the frame size changes, the grammar does not. Some of the rules of framing may vary, but the overall methods of composing shots in three dimensions remain the same.

The aspect ratio

The proportion of the frame is expressed as a ratio of width to height. This ratio is called the aspect ratio. The third dimension, depth, is a progression from the furthest distance to the closest distance and is known as backgrounds, middles and foregrounds, abbreviated to Bgd., Mgd. and Fgd., respectively.

The aspect ratio is normally given as a number to one, where the height is taken as unity (1). Thus, the aspect ratio for TV is 1.33:1; for cinema is 1.65:1; or for still photography is 1.50:1.

In more manageable units the aspect ratio for TV is expressed as 4:3. It is clear that a picture made in another aspect ratio does not fit the aspect ratio in which it is to be transmitted via television broadcasting. For example, a cinema film made 1.65:1 will lose 0.32 of its ratio, and consequently its picture, when shown on TV. In addition domestic television receivers, unlike precision studio monitors, are not always accurately aligned, so that a further area of picture will be lost when the picture is received 'at home'.

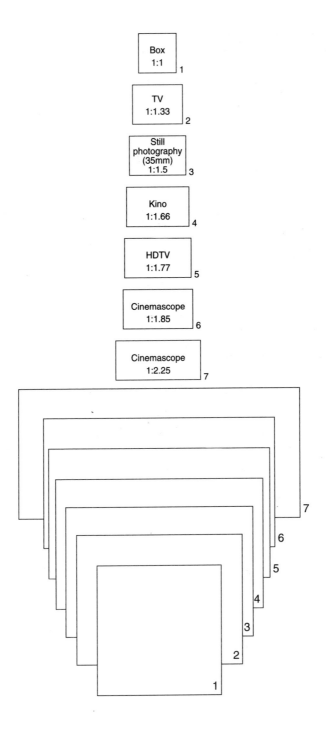

Box
1:1
1

TV
1:1.33
2

Still
photography
(35mm)
1:1.5
3

Kino
1:1.66
4

HDTV
1:1.77
5

Cinemascope
1:1.85
6

Cinemascope
1:2.25
7

7

6

5

4

3

2

1

Most countries have agreements as to what area of the aspect ratio can be said to be 'safe'. This safe area is expressed as a percentage of the transmitted area. For television in America for example, the safe area for screen action is 90%. A further 10% is considered needed to be safe for text, namely titles. Consequently, a cameraman must be aware that only 80 –90% of the screen is safe for home viewing and pictures must be composed with this in mind.

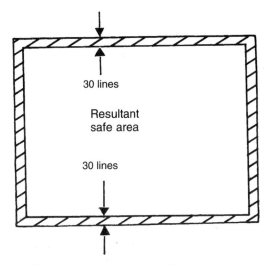

30 lines

Resultant
safe area

30 lines

10% is regarded as being
lost through misadjustment
of domestic TV receivers.

Also known as 'domestic cut-off'

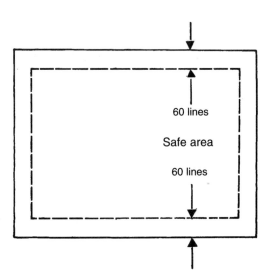

60 lines

Safe area

60 lines

A further 10% is lost to
ensure that essential action
and titles are within the final
safe area.

How do we see?

The line

'The line', is a joining of any two separated objects, people or things , which may be seen or unseen, between which an action may happen. It is an abstract concept which exists in the imagination of both the audience and the cameraman and is used as a gauge to associate those points.

'The line' is needed to:

- Clarify our viewing and to eliminate visual complications.
- Simplify the story to be told.
- Determine from where we, the audience, are looking.

The imaginary line can exist between two people looking at each other, or between a person looking at an object, between a person moving to an object or a place, or even between two places. The line can even exist between an object leaning or moving in one direction to another, in the way that the wind can blow a field of corn so that the stalks lean together in a certain direction.

Without 'the line' even the simplest scene can become confusing to an audience.

Example

A thief is running down the street with a stolen bag. There are two witnesses. The first witness, person A, saw the action from their window. The other witness, person B, watching from the opposite side of the street, also saw the thief run off. Diagram 1 shows a plan of the scene.

If the scene were to be made for pictures, and reconstructed directly from reality, then the two views would create confusion in the mind of the audience.

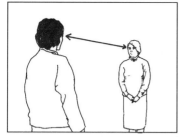

If two people look at each other it is an action. The line is between the two people.

Or between a man walking to a door.

Even close to the door there may still be a line.

Diagram 1

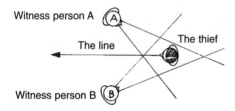

As seen by person A

As seen by person B

17

The confusion
Person A says that the robber escaped to their right (i.e. screen right), but person B says that the robber escaped to their left (i.e. screen left). The question is not whether person A or person B is correct. Both are correct. It is the difference in the two views that causes the confusion.

The solution
It is the task of the cameraman to eliminate confusion and to help make the story as clear as possible. Consequently, audience watching conventions, how the audience sees the scene, decrees that the view of the thief escaping, is shown either from an 'idealised' position of both witnesses or by omitting one witness position altogether.

In doing this, the story of the thief running down the street would still be the same, the cameraman simply having used film language to reinvent the 'truth' to fit the audience's understanding of the situation.

Applying 'the line'
The line, in this case, is the line of action of the thief. It is the direction in which he runs away and lies on the path of the escape.

In Diagram 2, the scene has been converted to film language and both the witnesses are located on one side of 'the line' only. It is clear that both the witnesses will see the robber escaping screen left, thus maintaining clarity of story telling without significantly altering the credibility.

The story has become more believable and logical to the viewer.

Thus 'the line', is critical as a guide for the audience. It helps to overcome the problem of credibility; it puts the audience in an idealised position so that they believe what they see. Otherwise 'reality' is not seen to be accurate.

THE SOLUTION

Diagram 2

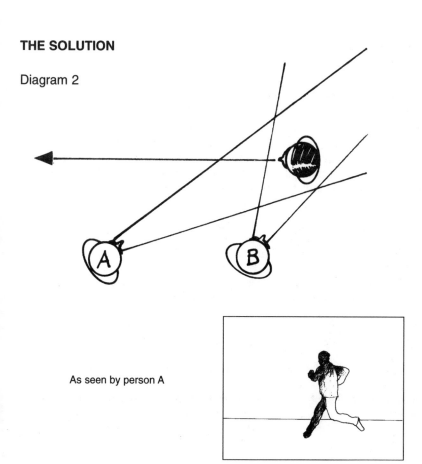

As seen by person A

As seen by person B

Objective and subjective shooting

There are two ways of seeing for shooting. They are called objective shooting and subjective shooting. Most camerawork is objective shooting.

Objective shooting
An objective shot is one which is made with impartial judgement or assessment. It exists independently in the perceiver's mind and is usually not distorted by personal emotions or prejudices. In objective shooting the camera is literally observing the scene, and can do so from as many viewpoints as required to tell the story of what is happening.

Example
Person A is in conversation with person B (see diagram). The scene is shot from position C, with shots of person A, of person B and perhaps both A and B together. There is no actual third person in the scene, even though the camera is acting as one. The audience views the scene from the point of view of a magical invisible person (at position C), who can see and hear, but can never touch or interfere with whatever is happening.

Subjective shooting
A subjective shot attempts to simulate views or feelings. It is not independent of the action, but attempts to be the action. In subjective shooting, the camera does not look at the scene, it is the scene.

Example
Person A is in conversation with person B. The camera takes the position of one of the persons and becomes them. In the diagram the camera has become person B, and the audience will see what person B would have seen. This would be a picture of person A, talking directly to the camera, because the camera is person B.

OBJECTIVE

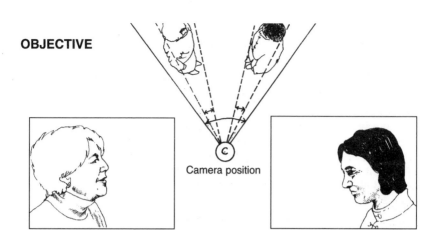

Person A as seen from position C

Camera position

Person B as seen from position C

A and B as seen from position C

SUBJECTIVE

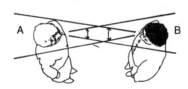

A   B

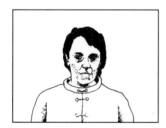

Person B as seen from person A

Person A as seen from person B

Because the camera is either person A or person B, there cannot be a true two shot in subjective shooting.

Objective and subjective mixed shooting

Often subjective and objective shots can be mixed. This is mostly in dramatic sequences but often occurs in a more simplified form when the audience (objective) needs to see what the subject sees (subjective).

Example

Person A is in conversation with person B and is shot objective in the normal way. Person A in the dialogue remarks on a building which is in his viewpoint (see diagram). If the audience has never previously seen the building, it will make the story clearer if the building is shown or seen from the point of view of person A. This is a subjective shot. It would edit easily into the objective scene.

Similar cases

Sometimes, seeing what the person is looking at could be either subjective or objective. This seems to be the case when that which is being looked at either has little perspective or is shaped in such a way that it looks similar from all viewpoints.

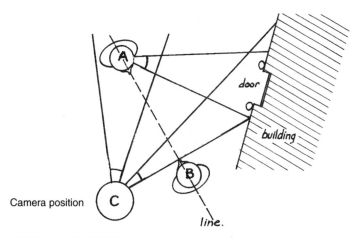

Camera position

MIXED SHOOTING

Person A talking to B
from position C
(objective)

He turns to look at the
building
(objective)

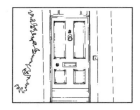

What person A sees
shot from A
(subjective)

Camara position as B
shooting person A
(subjective)

Person A turns to look
at the building
(subjective)

The building as seen
from position C
(objective)

Going from objective to subjective is often more convincing for an audience than subjective to objective.

23

Example
Persons A and B in conversation. The dialogue concerns the top of a large tower, as seen by person A. Obviously, unless there was something on the tower which could only be seen from the point of view of person A, then there is little difference between a shot taken from the position of person A and one taken from position C.

The need to provide shots either from objective or subjective viewpoints is to fulfil the visual needs of the audience. Failure to produce subjective viewpoints when they are referred to in the story, is to deny the audience information. Whilst this is acceptable in drama (to deny information in order to reveal it later), it is not acceptable in documentary where omission of visual or aural information would eventually lead to audience frustration.

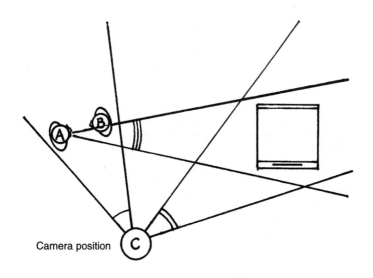

Camera position ⓒ

The tower as seen by A
(subjective)

The tower as seen from camera
position C
(objective)

Persons A and B as seen
from camera position C
(objective)

Elements of the shot

The shot

A shot is the basic division of a film or TV programme. In the same way as a play may be divided into scenes and acts, or an orchestral piece divided into parts and bars, a film or TV programme is divided up into scenes and shots. The shot is regarded as being the smallest possible unit when shooting.

The elements of the shot

A shot should have six important elements 'built in' to its manufacture. These six elements are necessary if the shot is to edit to the next shot in the programme. Even if the order of the shots, which shot follows which, is not known, the elements should still be included. Failure to do this may cause problems in the next stage of production which is editing.

Editing is the adjustment of words, pictures and sounds. It is the process of joining shots and scenes together. It is also part of the process of story telling. In moving pictures, the editing process puts the story together in a meaningful and believable way. Consequently, anything that is shot must be editable. Failure to fulfil editing requirements when shooting encourages disbelief and dissatisfaction in the mind of the audience.

The six elements are:

1. Motivation.
2. Information.
3. Composition.
4. Sound.
5. Camera angle.
6. Continuity.

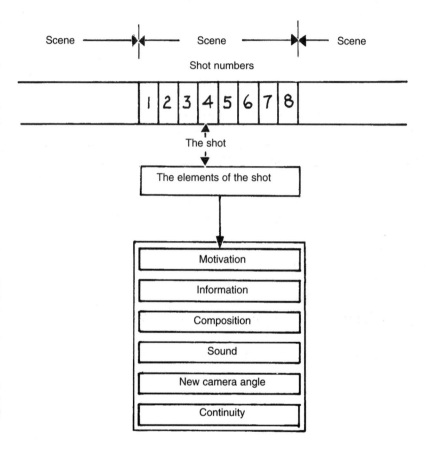

Scene ———►|◄——— Scene ———►|◄——— Scene

Shot numbers

| 1 | 2 | 3 | 4 | 5 | 6 | 7 | 8 |

The shot

The elements of the shot

Motivation

Information

Composition

Sound

New camera angle

Continuity

1 Motivation

Motivation is that part of the shot which gives the editor the reason, or motivation, to cut to another shot. Motivation can be in vision or in sound or a combination of the two. In drama shooting, the motivation is constructed, invented, as part of the story, but in documentary shooting, the motivation is often more difficult to see and shoot. Nevertheless, it is still there if observation and patience are encouraged.

Example
'The woman is sitting in a chair, silently reading a book.'

In documentary shooting this could be a single shot or a collection of shots, making up a small scene. The motivation must be something the audience can either see or hear. Consequently, if the shot takes in all the room, the motivation would have to be large enough to see. In such cases sound motivation is often more believable. A cough by another person, off shot, may be just sufficient for the subject to move her head or eyes in the direction of the sound. If it is a number of shots, the motivations are many. There may be a small movement of the body:

- a tiny scratch;
- a small movement of the hand;
- a shifting of the body;
- the turning of a page;
- the rubbing of the chin;
- the hand to the ear;
- the sniff of the nose;
- the blink of the eye;
- the movement of the eye;
- the movement of the foot;
- the straightening of the dress.

It is rare that any normal person is so completely still that no movement can be seen.

A small movement of the hand gives the motivation ...

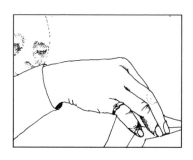

... to examine the hand more closely.

Turning the page allows the audience ...

... to see what sort of book she is reading.

A definite movement of the eye ...

... gives the audience the chance to see what she is looking at.

In drama shooting, motivations can be 'built in' as required. The motivation will follow the story, and the question can be asked, 'Why is the woman waiting?' This can be answered by a small head or eye movement to a clock on the wall. This would give a motivation to the editor to cut the next shot, which would be a shot of the clock that the woman was looking at. Dramatic motivations need not be large. The implication of the motivation is often more meaningful. For example, say the woman is reading, but waiting also. The sound of a door opening would be sufficient for the woman to react to and would give ample motivation for the reason for the reaction, which is the next shot, of a person opening the door.

The woman is waiting. A small movement of the eye ...

means the editor can cut to the clock ...

A woman is reading. The *sound* of the door opening makes her look up ...

and another person enters the room.

Or alternatively:

Woman is reading, sound of door,

another enters,

then she looks up.

2 Information

Each shot should have new information for the audience, which should be additional to the last piece of information. The audience needs this additional information, both visual and aural, if the story to be told is to develop, or if it is to create curiosity. Created curiosity should, in turn, be satisfied or withheld, as in drama. In vision, new information can often mean added detail, or another way of looking at the same thing.

Example
'The woman is sitting in a chair, silently reading a book.'

By showing a series of successive pictures, each with new information, the audience's detailed knowledge of the scene increases.

- Who is the woman?
- How does she sit?
- How old is she?
- What does she look like?
- What is the book? Is it well used? Paperback or hardback?
- Where is the room?
- Is there a window?
- What is seen through it?
- What is heard through the window?
- What is heard in the room?
- What else is in the room?
- What time of day or night is it in the room.

The woman is not in isolation, but is surrounded by an environment, both in vision or in sound or in both. All these small seemingly insignificant, trifles will contribute to the audience's understanding of the scene.

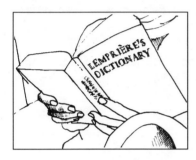

This gives information about the book she is reading.

Tells you how old she is – what her face looks like.

Tells you about what is outside the room.

3 Composition

A shot is composed. Composition is made up of:

- framing;
- the illusion of depth;
- the subjects or objects within the frame.

Items 2 (depth) and 3 (subjects or objects) can be enhanced by the use of colour.

Framing

A frame is a limit to a view. So framing, by limiting the view, isolates it and thereby draws attention to it (see aspect ratio). It is a significant factor in composition, and has, over the years, become standardised. Framing is initially concerned with two dimensions only.

Depth

On a two-dimensional screen, depth is obviously an illusion. It is made up of the following conventions (see overleaf also):

- convergence;
- relative size;
- density;
- juxtaposition;
- colour.

Subjects or objects

The placing and the movement of the subjects or objects within a frame is also based on convention. It comes from the history of painting and the history of standardisation of the film industry, mainly Hollywood.

As audiences have learned to 'read' these conventions, it is necessary to be aware of them and apply them if the audience is to understand the picture for the message or story intended.

Colour

Colour can be the composition in itself or it can also be used to emphasise composition based on monochrome design.

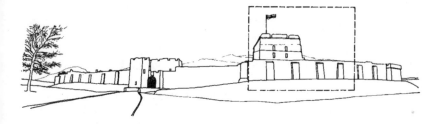

Framing is isolating a view.

Arranging the framing to help create an illusion of depth.

And the placing of subject(s) within the frame.

4 Sound

Sound differs from vision in one most important way. In vision, the eyes choose what they see. With sound, the ears have no choice. Also, sound is more immediate than vision, and, as it is more abstract, it produces a picture in the mind more suited to the individual person's expectation than does vision.

Sound is a primary experience. Like taste or smell, it is difficult to describe by words, or by vision or by using the other senses as a reference. Consequently, sound can exist on its own, but pictures hardly ever.

Experienced sound recordists and sound editors have a very important saying: 'You don't have to see what you hear, but you have to hear what you see!'

Whatever is seen on the screen, normally should also be heard on the screen. But something can be heard on the screen without it being seen. Nearly all situations seen will also have their own sound, even when there seems to be none.

A computer keyboard seen to be working must be *heard* to be working.

A train pulling out of a station must be *heard* as a train pulling out of a station. Extra station sounds can be heard but need not be seen.

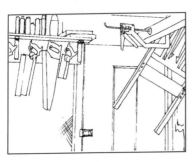

But if a sound is heard that we don't recognise then eventually we have to show it. 'Thonk … thonk … thonk'

… thonk … thonk … thonk.
The picture finally explains the sound.

Example
'The woman is waiting.'

Say, for example the scene is set in a quiet house in a quiet street in a small town. The number of sounds would be extensive.

- The woman has a sound; her breathing or even her heartbeat.
- Her clothes have a sound. Silk makes a different sound from leather.
- Her skin has a sound. If she rubs her hands together, dry skin has a different sound to wet skin, and the way in which skin is rubbed makes for different sounds.
- The chair in which she is sitting may make a sound.
- The room has its own sound. This sound is called atmosphere in the room, known as atmo or atmos.
- There will be a sound, however faint, outside the room. It may be other types of atmos. It may be the sound of the street or of the traffic.
- There may be the sound of an individual item or thing in the room. A clock may have a particular tick. A cat can have an individual purr.

Whatever the vision there will be the appropriate sound.

In cases where an unusual or unrecognisable sound is heard but not initially seen, then it is important for the audience to eventually see what is making the sound.

The woman has a sound ... perhaps the sound of breath.

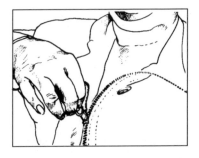

Leather has a sound, especially the zip.

Skin sound.

Atmosphere of the room.

Traffic outside the window has a sound.

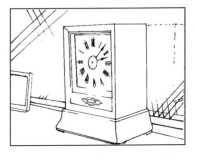

A clock may have a certain tick sound.

5 Camera angle

The term camera angle describes the position from which we, the audience, are looking at the object or subject. Each new shot should have a new camera angle. There are three reasons for this:

1. To increase the possibility of new information.
2. To increase the possibility of shots editing together.
3. To copy more closely how people react to new subjects or objects.

When seeing somebody or something for the first time we tend to alter our viewpoints so that we more closely observe what it is we are looking at. It is similar with the selection of the camera angles. A number of factors affect this choice. These factors are:

- the types of shot being used;
- the framing of the shot;
- the background in the frame;
- the illusion of depth in the shot;
- the colour and light in the shot;
- the sound in the shot.

Some subjects may be shot from almost any angle, whilst other subjects will best be seen from only a limited number of angles.

Camera angle is referred to in degrees (see diagram). The two rules written in the early days of film making are still valid for the novice cameraman of today.

The 180 degree rule

This rule effectively said that the action of the subject or subjects is the centre of a circle and that the diameter of that circle passes through the action, and shooting is permitted within 180 degrees of one side of the circle only (see diagram).

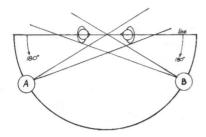

180° rule
Two shots taken, one from position A and one from position B, i.e. from the same side of the circle, are permissible, because they can be edited together.

Shot taken from A

Shot taken from B

The result is that the two people are looking at each other.

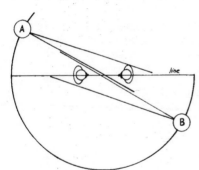

If A is taken from one side of the circle, but B is taken from the opposite side of the circle (crossing the line), the result is different.

Shot taken from A

Shot taken from B

This result has a different meaning – that two people are looking at a third (not seen).

The 30 degree rule

When taking shots of the action within the 180 degree rule, the camera should be placed never less than 30 degrees from the last position of the camera (see diagram).

Whilst the 180 degree and the 30 degree rules are still fundamentally correct today, it is understood that the position of the half-circle can change within a scene and consequently, there are ways to shoot from both sides of the circle. The 30 degree rule is still basic practice, even though the angle can sometimes be smaller.

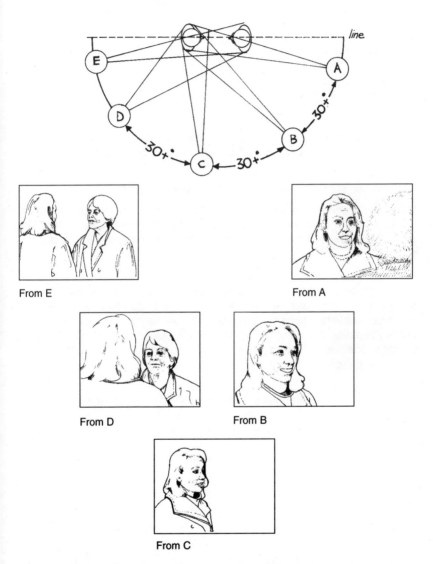

From E

From A

From D

From B

From C

Shots taken less than 30° from each other should be significantly different from each other if they are to give any additional information to the audience. For example, A is significantly different from E but not from B. B is not that different from C but it is from D.

6 Continuity

Continuity is maintaining the established flow of visual and aural production detail between takes, shots and scenes. There are five main parts to continuity:

1. Content continuity.
2. Movement continuity.
3. Position continuity.
4. Sound continuity.
5. Dialogue continuity.

Content continuity

Content continuity covers all visual elements concerned with the shot. These range from people and properties to dress and make-up.

Example

'The woman is sitting in a chair, silently reading a book.'

When the scene is shot with a number of shots, and has to appear continuous in time, then the visual elements in the shot remain the same. The same book, the same clothes and hair style. The same chair and ornaments.

Movement continuity

The majority of shots contain movement of one form or another, even though it may be small. But a small movement becomes a big movement close up; consequently, being aware of the movement and its direction is critical, because movements may have to be repeated in another shot within that scene. Movement must be carefully observed in order that it matches that in the previous shot.

Position continuity

Position continuity is the position of the subject or object within the screen. If a subject is positioned at the right-hand side of the screen in the first shot then they must be on the same side in the following shot, and cannot be on the left-hand side.

When the subject is the same, then the continuity of the arm movement must be similar in both shots.

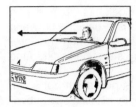

The direction of the movement must also be similar.

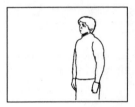

The position of the subject in the screen must be similar.

Even when there is no movement of an object, position continuity must be similar.

If the continuity of position is reversed the eye will JUMP between the two shots from A to B.

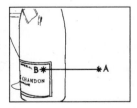

If two shots, when edited together, are to appear continuous then position continuity must be maintained; otherwise the eyes of the audience jump from one side of the screen to the other. Position continuity also applies to objects.

Sound continuity
The continuity of sound is also critical. Not only in relevance to foreground or background position but in its perspective. Sound continuity holds the audience's attention. The audience expects that the ticking of a clock seen on a mantelpiece which is distinctly heard in one shot, will be heard in the following shot. If it does not, then it means that the clock has stopped, and dramatically this can have another meaning. There is a balance between foreground dialogue and background sound, but even though the foreground dialogue or sound may be new in a following shot, the background sound must remain.

Sound continuity applies even when the sound is heard but not seen. The audience will still require the same sound in the following or subsequent shots to match that in the first one. The only exceptions to this fundamental requirement are when the following occur.

■ The sound is heard to change and there is a shot in vision to show why the change has happened. For example, changing from a town location to a country location.
■ The change in sound is clear in its meaning. For example, the sound of an aircraft landing changes to the sound of aircraft tyres screeching on the airport runway.

Change of continuity
All the types of continuity are common in one aspect, in that they cannot change unless:

■ it is seen to change on screen as part of the 'story'; or
■ there is an apparent time interval between two shots, during which continuity might have changed.

Other than for these two exceptions, continuity must be maintained for each shot.

The sound of a computer keyboard will continue from one shot into the next shot.

If an aircraft is heard and seen in the first shot then it will still be heard in the next shot even though it can't be seen.

Equipment used

The shot is determined by its content (the subject) and by the characteristics and use of the equipment, usually:

- the pan and tilt head;
- the camera support;
- the lens.

The use of the equipment is determined by how much it must move or not move.

Developments in equipment

In the early days of photography, the subject, the person who was having his picture taken, could not move. This was because of long exposure times due to insensitive film. With the invention of the moving picture camera, technology had progressed sufficiently enough to allow for subject movement. But it was still not possible to move the apparatus, which is why all the shots had a static frame and the actors moved within it.

Next, the panning head, a device to swivel the camera from side to side, was developed. Now the camera could follow action from right to left and back.

Next, the camera and its support was put on wheels, so that the entire position of the camera and all its accompanying apparatus could be moved along a row of 'tracks'.

In recent times the zoom lens was invented. This allowed the focal length of a lens and hence the framing to be altered. With the continuing development and refinement of technology, moving shots have become more fluid, more realistic and more natural.

The equipment

Introduction

The design and development of the equipment used by the camera operator is related to human equivalents. It is the nature of man that he can adjust his viewpoint by a combination of eye and of body movement. His eyes swivel and can focus by selection. His head can turn through nearly 180 degrees, and by turning his body more rotation gan be gained. The body can do all these movements smoothly and unobtrusively.

Although all camera shots, by the nature of the apparatus, are an artificial way of recording visuals, some shots and movements appear more convincing than others because they more closely resemble the way human beings see.

It is not an accident, therefore, that the design and use of the apparatus should emulate human movement in that camera movement should be smooth and unobtrusive.

The pan and tilt head
A pan is a pivotal movement of a camera in a horizontal plane. A tilt is a pivotal movement in the vertical plane. The pan and tilt head is a device sited between the camera and the camera support which allows for controlled pivotal movements in either plane or in a combination of planes.

It is sometimes referred to as the panning head, friction head, free head or simply the head, and is fitted firmly both to the camera above it and to the camera support (tripod etc.) below it.

The camera mounting
The purpose of a camera mount is:

- To hold the camera and head at the position required with the maximum possible rigidity.
- To facilitate the movement of the camera and head from one place to another.

Any evidence of unwanted movement, shake or drift in the shot has the effect of distracting the audience from the story being told. Distractions take many forms, but the worst of all are shots which bring attention to themselves because they are not steady.

Lightweight pan and tilt head

Geared head

Studio head

Pan

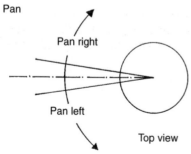

Pan right

Pan left

Top view

Tilt

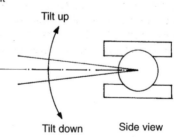

Tilt up

Tilt down

Side view

Unsteady shots are caused either by not using a camera mounting, by using the wrong mounting or by using the right mounting in the wrong way. Mountings come in various shapes and sizes and range from the very sophisticated to the very simple.

Tripod: A three-legged support, adjustable in height, which is fixed prior to the shot.

Baby tripod: A smaller version of the tripod.

High hat: A fixed support of three very short parallel legs fixed directly to the floor and used for very low camera shots.

Spider: A device with three arms for making the feet of the tripod more stable.

Skid (rolling spider): A spider with small wheels on it.

Pedestal: A hydraulic device for lifting and lowering the camera based around a telescopic central cylinder. The pedestal can be steered by a tiller in a fixed or a flexible route. Sometimes the pedestal is adjustable to be run on tracks.

Tracks: Parallel rails which can be fixed together to run in curved or straight routes.

Flat bed: A flat tray or truck which supports a tripod and runs on tracks.

Dolly: A wheeled mounting that allows for movement in the height of the camera via cranked arms and for movement of the entire apparatus in any direction. The dolly has greater height possibilities than the pedestal. Usually motorised, the speed of the dolly can be accurately controlled.

Crane: A larger dolly supporting a long boom, on the end of which the camera and head are mounted. The elevation of the camera can be up to 20 feet.

Cherry picker: A boom mounted on a wagon which can extend to a height greater than the crane.

Pedestal boom: A small boom which can be mounted on a pedestal.

Tripod and baby.
The pan and tilt head
fits either.

High hat. The pan and
tilt head sits on this and
is even lower than a
baby.

Spider. Holds the tripod
steady especially on
polished surfaces. Also
known as a 'spreader'.

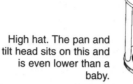

Skid. For rolling around
on highly smooth floors.

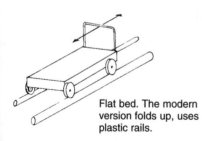

Pedestal

Dolly

Crane

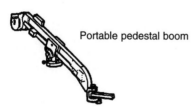

Flat bed. The modern
version folds up, uses
plastic rails.

Portable pedestal boom

Monorail: A single rail of great flexibility on to which the camera is hung.

Steadicam: The trade name of a device which, when fitted to the cameraman's body, can hold the camera steady in positions and situations where other types of mountings cannot be used.

Clamps: Devices to make the camera steady when attached to cars, buildings etc. by use of screw fixings or limpet attachments. The limpet attachment is often called a suction head.

Unorthodox mountings: Any platform or stable surface which can rigidly support a camera. These could include tables, chairs, boxes etc. Used only in an emergency and in the absence of other mountings more suitable.

Shoulder mounting: The most unstable of all mountings. Used principally for news where the cameraman's flexibility and speed of movement may be more important than perfection in framing.

The lens

The lens is a device, usually of glass, which causes a beam of light rays to converge or diverge on passing through it. In the early days of cameras, lenses were relatively crude devices compared to todays' and were of a fixed focal length. To change a focal length meant having a set of lenses. Today the set of lenses is encased in one single device called a zoom lens. This is a set of fixed focal length lenses, however infinite the range. The word 'zoom' refers to changing from one focal length to another.

Some contemporary practices include the action of the zoom as being the shot itself. But this practice should not be encouraged. If one of the principles of good camerawork is never to draw the attention of the audience to the camera movement itself, then the practice of zooming breaks this principle because it is a highly artificial way of recording a picture.

The zoom lens is an important development of modern camera technology. Used correctly, it enlarges the possibilities of shooting. Used incorrectly, it draws attention to the technology and not to the shot.

Limpet – a suction attachment for flat surfaces.

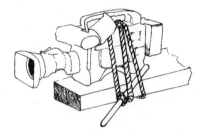

Unorthodox – here a tourniquet holds a camera in a fixed position.

Shoulder mount – News use; notice how the cameraman tries to be his own tripod.

Types of shot

The types of shot available

There are only three types of shot, classified according to movement or non-movement of the apparatus. They are described as:

1. Simple shots.
2. Complex shots.
3. Developing shots.

The types of shot differ from each other according to which of the following four items move (see overleaf):

- the subject,
- the lens,
- the pan and tilt head,
- the camera mounting.

There are variations of the types of shots, and new ways of shooting are constantly being tried and developed.

The simple shot
This is a shot composed of a subject(s) or object(s) made without movement of the lens, the pan and tilt head or the camera mounting.

Simple means 'singular' not 'easy'. It is the most commonly used shot and is often the most effective in story telling. As there is no technical movement, all the attention of the audience is drawn to the activity within the frame.

There are around twelve commonly used simple shots, but over fifty variations of them. The classification of the individual simple shots is based on the relation of the human figure to the frame. This relationship is established in 'shot composition'. Consequently, framing, position of subject, perspective, colour etc. become essential.

The composition of shots is a fundamental activity in the work of the cameraman.

SHOT TYPE | THAT WHICH CAN MOVE

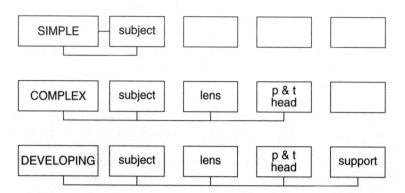

SIMPLE	subject			

COMPLEX	subject	lens	p & t head	

DEVELOPING	subject	lens	p & t head	support

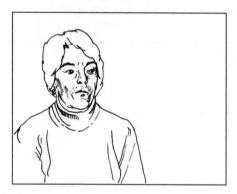

A simple shot may have a static or moving subject but there is no planned movement of the frame.

A simple shot may be of an object or objects. There is no movement of the frame.

57

The complex shot

This is a shot composed of a moving subject(s) or object(s) made with movement of either the lens or the pan and tilt head, or both.

Complex means 'consisting of several closely connected parts'. In the complex shot there are five closely connecting parts: subject movement, lens focus movement, change in the lens focal length (lens angle), panning movement and tilting movement. The movement can be either singular or in any combination.

The developing shot

This is a shot composed of a subject(s) or object(s) made with movement either of subject(s), lens, camera pan and tilt head and camera mounting, or all.

Developing means the act of starting with one thing and changing to another. In the developing shot the viewpoint is in one position and shifts to another with or without the subject.

As the variation of movement is limitless, the developing shot differs from the complex shot in that the camera mounting moves from one place to another. Consequently, the change in background, as the viewpoint changes, becomes much more important.

Movement descriptions

The descriptions of camera movements have to be precise. In different countries there are some variations of terms often due to language or trade names of the equipment used. Also some equipment has its own operating terms. Thus a jib arm mounted on a pedestal cannot pan left, it must jib left. The term pan refers to the pivotal action only of the pan and tilt head. Technically speaking, a pedestal cannot 'crane up', but a crane can etc.

A professional has to understand and use the operational terms of the equipment in production.

Shot definitions

Shot definitions are divided into either, those related to people in the frame or those related to objects in the frame.

There is a historic relationship between framing of people and objects and the history of painting. Many of our principles of framing in film and TV are based on inventions, discoveries and conventions from past cultures, and the principles laid down by a Renaissance mathematician, Lucas Pacioli, (devina proportione) still hold good today.

The conventions of shot names have a precise meaning and have very few variable factors. Variations or modifications to the shot are often required and it is sometimes the variations which give special meaning to the shot, even though the name of the shot does not change. No shot is absolute, especially those which show people. Whilst the conventions are known internationally, their names are not. In the USA, the medium long shot is referred to as the knee shot; the same shot in Germany is known as the American knee shot or 'the American' for short, whilst in Sri Lanka it is called a half Kingsley, after the name of the first cinema (Kingsley) in Colombo. To overcome confusion, some cameramen even refer to body areas, e.g. 'a bust shot' is a medium close up. Here, European terms are used.

Framing
Framing is the process of selecting a part of a view in order to isolate it and so give it emphasis. In film and TV usage, it is a horizontal rectangular frame, the sides of which are defined (in TV) as a ratio of 3:4 or 1:1.33.

Composition
Composition is the arrangement of the objects and/or people within the frame. Its use in film and TV is to create the third dimension, namely depth, within the frame.

Framing is selective.

Composition is the arrangement of the subject(s) within the frame. By selective framing a new story can be invented or even a story within a story.

Framing is part of composition. Other elements of composition are objects in relationship to each other, perspective, colour, object or subject movement, shape, form and direction.

Subject position

Subject refers to anything that is being shot. But 'subject position' refers mainly to people. There are three main reference positions of a single subject, though if more than one person is in the frame, the subject positions can be different and can alter. The three main subject reference positions are:

Direct to camera
Three-quarters profile
Profile

Direct to camera

This position is used when a person has a communication with the camera. The communication can be with eyes, gestures, movements or words. It is called a 'subjective shot', because the relationship of the person in frame is with YOU the observer through the lens, or YOU the observer of the screen. It is the position of a person in the frame whose eyes are looking directly at the camera. It is often achieved when the person faces the camera, but also has a variation called 'controposto'.

Three-quarters profile

The subject is looking at someone or something. Gestures, movements of eyes or dialogue with words are related to another person or object which may or may not be in the frame. It is called an 'objective shot' because the camera is observing the subject who is observing another subject.

Profile

The subject may look into or out of the frame. There may be more than one person in the frame. It is also an objective shot, because the camera is observing.

SUBJECT POSITION
How the subject is positioned relative to the camera

| Direct to camera | ¾ Profile | Profile |

Subjective   Objective   Objective

Mixed subject reference positions

When there are a number of people in the frame, they can also be shot with mixed reference positions. This was very common in the history of painting and in early photography. Mixed subject reference positions developed 'eye lines' or 'eye directions' within the group, aided composition and often made the 'story' within the picture. The positioning of people within a frame is a skill which must be learnt; without it, composition of groups can be mundane and unconvincing.

Headroom

Headroom is the distance between the top of the subjects head and the top of the frame. It is a fixed amount for a certain size of shot. As a shot size changes, according to how close the subject is in the frame, then the headroom changes, until it disappears altogether in closer shots. Shots made for film have a different headroom to those made for TV.

In addition, domestic TV receivers reduce the total amount of the picture area by 5%, so that the correct headroom in a camera viewfinder may appear incorrect at home. This loss of area is called 'domestic cut-off'. A cameraman must allow a little more headroom to compensate for this.

Noseroom

Noseroom, often called 'looking room', is the distance between the eye which is furthest away from the camera and the edge of the frame to which the person is looking. Noseroom can be either right or left frame. The use of this space is not only psychological, it is also an optical requirement to ready the eye to move to another view. Noseroom, like headroom, varies according to the size of the shot.

Footroom

This is the space, on some of the wider shots, between the feet of the subject and the lower edge of the frame.

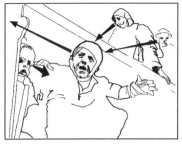

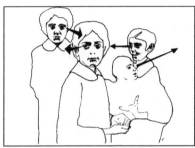

Mixed subject reference positions.

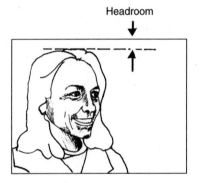

Headroom

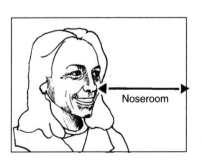

Headroom

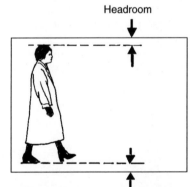

Headroom on a shot of a complete person – there would also be room at the feet (foot room).

Noseroom

Noseroom

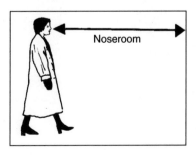

65

Simple shots

There are nine simple shots of the single person, of which seven are very common, but there are over fifty variations of them. All of the simple shots refer to looking at people from the height of the eyes of the person being observed. The simple shots are known as:

- extreme long shot,
- very long shot,
- long shot,
- medium long shot,
- medium shot,
- medium close-up,
- close-up,
- big close-up,
- extreme close-up.

Abbreviations

It is normal for cameramen to abbreviate the names of shots. Also abbreviated is the position from where they shoot. High angle (H/A) is shot from higher than the subject's eyes. Low angle (L/A) is shot from below the subject's eyes. Consequently, a medium close-up shot from a high angle of a man called Theodore would be abbreviated to H/A MCU Theo.

Extreme long shot: XLS/ELS

Medium shot: MS

Very long shot: VLS

Medium close-up: MCU

Long shot: LS

Close-up: CU

Medium long shot: MLS

Big close-up: BCU

Extreme close-up: XCU/ECU

67

SHOT: EXTREME LONG SHOT
Abbreviation: XLS or ELS
Subject position: Not applicable

FRAMING	The subject is so small in the frame that it is totally unrecognisable. The figure is less than one-sixth of the height of the frame. It is possible to tell if the subject is human, but not possible to tell if the subject is male or female.
COMPOSITION	This shot takes in a massive area both in framing (height and width) and in pictorial composition, where the depth of field might run to infinity, e.g. where the horizion can be in focus as well as the immediate foreground. The XLS can convey atmosphere and environment. The golden mean can be applied in the positioning of figures or subjects.
PROBLEMS	The position of a figure in the frame, right or left, is critical because of the space around the figure. There are no problems with domestic cut-off. Some problems can be encountered in using the lens at its widest angle, because distortion (of verticals) occurs.
USE	This shot is often used in opening sequences where recognition of the scene is more important than recognition of a person or of persons. The shot is used to convey 'where', but it cannot show 'who'. It is a shot that is used for a wealth of general information without showing detail. Often used as an introduction to setting of the scene.
NOTES	This shot is also known as the wide angle or wide shot and, because the majority of the frame is taken up with the scene rather than a person, it is sometimes known as the geography shot.

XLS or ELS
Extreme long shot

SHOT: VERY LONG SHOT
Abbreviation: VLS
Subject position: Not applicable

FRAMING	The subject is about one-third of the height of the frame and is now recognisable as to clothing and gender. Some activity can be seen but not recognised. The majority of the frame is still concerned with geography and environment. Headroom and footroom causes no problems.
COMPOSITION	The composition can be developed in many ways especially in movement of the subject. In the VLS, a figure can be taken easily from background to foreground. Most suited of all the shots to composing according to the golden mean.
PROBLEMS	The main problem is a subject moving right or left. The head is so small in the frame that eyelines are impossible to determine, and consequently body direction in movement is more likely. Depending on the lens angle chosen, vertical proportions may be distorted, as in the XLS, but this can be overcome by shooting on a narrower lens angle.
USE	Used widely where recognition of the figure is needed without the recognition of the individual person. It is applied in opening sequences, where the figure and its movement are of near equal importance as the background.
NOTES	Loss of picture due to domestic cut-off is minimal, but action shot near the edge of the frame can be lost.

VLS
Very long shot

SHOT: LONG SHOT
Abbreviation: LS
Subject position: Three-quarters profile, profile, direct to camera

FRAMING	The subject with headroom and footroom covers the entire frame from top to bottom. The clothing is more recognisable as is gender. As the figure covers only approximately one-sixth of the area of the screen, then there is still a great emphasis on the background area and environment.
	The figure is now large enough for any subject action to be clearly seen, so the audience's attention begins to be drawn to the foreground figure. In this shot, examination of detail is not possible. Head movement is clearly seen so that eyes can be identified if there is a single figure only. Where two or more figures are in shot, the eye lines between them are less obvious.
COMPOSITION	Composition must be such that the audience's attention is either drawn to the environment or to the person or to a combination of both.
PROBLEMS	In the LS the audience has to decide if the story takes place in the foreground or the background. This shot can rarely be used as an introductory shot.
EXCEPTIONS	Where the environment is already known to the audience, e.g. soaps.
USE	Often used with a moving person, e.g. a subject walking, running, moving hands etc.
NOTES	No significant loss due to domestic cut-off. The position of the figure in the frame, screen right or left, is critical to allow for body movement.

LS
Long shot
Direct to camera

LS
Long shot
Profile

LS
Long shot, low angle (LA)
Direct to camera

SHOT: MEDIUM LONG SHOT
Abbreviation: MLS
Subject position: Direct to camera

FRAMING	This is the first of the shots where the subject's body is cut by the frame. In this shot the subject is framed with headroom and is cut with the lower frame either above or below the knee. The choice, above or below the knee, depends upon the sex and clothing of the subject and the speed of movement, if any. Often the deciding factor with women is the length of the dress. If the subject is stationary the shot is framed above the knee, and when moving framed below the knee.
	The subject is close enough to be able to recognise the type of clothes, colour and general conditions. Hair and skin tones can be recognised, but not details. Facial changes can be seen, but not detailed. The figure covers about one-quarter of the width of the screen.
COMPOSITION PROBLEMS	This shot gives lots of variations on composition. The eye movement is not clear enough to be used as the motivation for a directional edit.
USE	Widely used, especially where direction, using arm movement, is included in the shot.
NOTES	Framing an MLS using a narrow angle lens limits the depth of field but has an advantage in story telling in that it draws the attention of the audience completely to the foreground.

MLS
Medium long shot
Direct to camera

MLS
Medium long shot
Low angle

SHOT: MEDIUM SHOT
Abbreviation: MS
Subject position: Direct to camera

FRAMING	Headroom is standard on the upper frame. The lower frame cuts below the waist and below the elbow. The waistline can be seen which allows for twisting movements of the body. Eye movement can be clearly seen. The approximate age of the person can be determined, the hair colour and if they are wearing a certain type of glasses. It is also possible to determine costume texture.
COMPOSITION	Attention is clearly drawn to the figure rather than the background. This is because the subject's eyes can be fully seen and therefore the eyeline of the subject draws the attention of the audience. Body movement is only partial within this shot, e.g. if the subject is framed screen left or right, an arm movement would probably mean the hand touching the edge of the screen, and breaking the composition.
PROBLEMS	Breaking composition.
EXCEPTIONS	Scenes where the action is so fast that breaks in composition are not noticed because of the action of the subjects.
USE	Mainly with subjects with limited movement.
NOTES	Providing the background does not detract, it is possible to recognise some facial movement.

MS
Medium shot
Objective

MS
Medium shot, high angle
Subjective

MS
Medium shot, low angle
Subjective

77

SHOT: MEDIUM CLOSE-UP
Abbreviation: MCU
Subject position: Direct to camera

FRAMING

Normal headroom with the lower frame cutting the subject below the arm joint (armpit) or below the breast pocket in a jacket-wearing male or on the chest contour on a female. In both male and female the lower frame cuts above the elbow. Variations in shooting females depend upon clothing, e.g. 'V' necks. For obvious reasons, care must be taken when framing females wearing strapless gowns.

Facial expression is predominant and the subject's eyeline is obvious. Skin tone is becoming recognisable, as is the appearance of skin blemishes. Also, discrepancies in certain facial movements of the subject become very obvious, e.g. the eyes can appear to be of different sizes.

COMPOSITION

Attention is completely drawn to the face and the background is virtually forgotten. The eyes lie on the upper two-thirds line. There is still space for another activity or part of an activity to be seen in the background, but the opportunities are limited. It is mostly a foreground shot. The hair-style and hair texture can clearly be seen on the MCU, as can cosmetics. Lighting reflections can become noticeable on the brow of a male subject but this is less likely on a female one, depending on hair-style.

PROBLEMS

The main problem is with the subject's eyes: without extra lighting, or lighting reflectors, the eyes can seem flat and lifeless.

USE

Very common in all forms of production, as the shot is close enough to tell the audience all about the subject but without getting too close so that the shot becomes intrusive or unreal.

MCU
Medium close-up
Direct to camera

MCU
Medium close-up, high angle
Direct to camera

MCU
Medium close-up, low angle
Direct to camera

SHOT: CLOSE-UP
Abbreviation: CU
Subject position: Direct to camera

FRAMING	The lower frame should cut the subject's torso in the area from above the arm joint to below the chin, so that some of the subject's shoulder is shown. The upper frame may cut the head or may not, depending upon the gender and hair-style of the subject.
COMPOSITION	The attention of the viewer is drawn to the fore-ground only, focused on the subject's eyes and mouth. Skin colour and texture can be clearly seen, but not eye colour without either special make-up or lighting. Eyes at this stage are either light or dark. With a male it is possible to tell skin condition, and if they have shaved or not. Hair texture is obvious in the female as is hair condi-tion.
PROBLEMS	Framing the shot without a part of the shoulder showing means that the lower frame cuts the neck. This has the effect of the subject appearing to be dismembered from their body.
	Problems in headroom can also arise. A minimal headroom can be lost completely after domestic cut-off, which will result in a badly framed shot or, if no headroom is allowed, the resultant shot may appear to be tight in the frame.
USE	To see this framing in normal life, the viewer and the subject would have to be very close to each other. This shot would therefore be used in equiv-alent circumstances, such as a love scene, telling a secret or a scene showing anger.

80

CU
Close-up
Direct to camera

CU
Close-up, high angle
Direct to camera

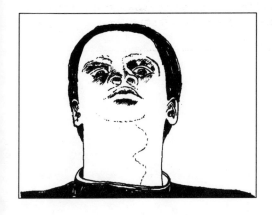

CU
Close-up, low angle
Direct to camera

81

SHOT: BIG CLOSE-UP
Abbreviation: BCU
Subject position: Direct to camera

FRAMING	The upper frame cuts the subject's brow. The lower frame edge cuts usually above the chin. Skin tissue can clearly be seen, together with any deformities. Eyebrow hair becomes predominant, as do eyelids. Eye direction is massive and mouth distortions become unreal because of size. Any face movement on this shot is consequently overemphasised because it becomes unrealistic on screen.
COMPOSITION	No composition whatsoever.
PROBLEMS	Any movement of the subject, however slight, becomes massive movement on screen. There are therefore significant problems of maintaining framing if the subject moves. Focus also becomes a major problem, as the depth of field can be so small that the slightest movement can displace focus and give the appearance of the focus going 'soft'.
	The nose, mouth and eyes of the subject are so large that their proportion, in relation to the shots of the same subject that come before or after it, become difficult to edit together convincingly.
USE	This shot is so close that it can only be used in situations of emotion, such as a love scene or an aggressive scene.

BCU
Big close-up
Direct to camera

SHOT: EXTREME CLOSE-UP
Abbreviation: XCU or ECU
Subject position: Direct to camera

FRAMING	The framing of this shot concentrates on one or sometimes two features; eyes or eyes and nose, nose and mouth or mouth alone. Emphasis on the eyes clearly shows the colour.
COMPOSITION	No composition.
PROBLEMS	The depth of field is so small that focus position is critical and must be carefully chosen. For example, the focus set on the eyes could mean that the focus is likely to be soft on the nose. Depending upon the type of lens used and the lens angle, even the focus difference between the eyelashes and the eyeball may be evident. Eye movement is enormous.

Any subject movement becomes a problem in both focusing and framing. The loss of subject due to domestic cut-off is very predominant.

There are probably more problems than opportunities with this shot. Incorrectly used, this shot misleads the viewer, because it totally isolates one part of the subject and makes nearly any subject sinister, aggressive and nasty. The shot lacks dignity.

USE	Very limited use in dramatic work, the shot is mostly used in educational TV or in medical programmes.

Sometimes it can be seen in badly made kung fu films or in early spaghetti westerns.

XCU or ECU
Extreme close-up

Shot variations

The three-quarters profile

The three-quarters profile is an objective shot of a subject looking or talking to a another person not in vision, or to an object which may or may not be in vision. Because of the way in which one objective shot is edited to another, the position of the subject within the frame during a three-quarters profile shot is much more important than in the direct to camera position or subjective shot.

In this shot, the space between the eyes and the edge of the frame to which the subject is looking is a crucial measurement if the shot is to be convincing to the audience. For example, there is little reason to shoot a subject in three-quarters profile in a very long shot framing, as the audience are not likely to see the eyes of the subject. Consequently, the three-quarters profile is normally used in long shot framing and closer shots.

The subject is positioned within one side of the frame and the choice of shot generally depends upon the importance of an eye movement and any gesture the subject may make. An arm movement, for example an outstretched arm and pointing finger, cannot be shot on a three-quarter profile medium close-up, as the hand will appear to be amputated by the edge of the frame, and must therefore be shot using either MS, MLS or LS framing.

Eye direction is obviously much stronger in MCU and closer, but the space left for gesture is very much reduced, and limited to those closer to the face of the subject. Thus, stroking the chin would be acceptable on three-quarters profile MCU, but not on a CU framing, again because of the amputation effect and an unconnected hand appearing from the lower edge of the frame.

The position of the eyes in the MCU, CU and BCU is measured as follows: the eye which is furthest away from the camera, lies on the vertical centre line of the picture. For shots wider than MCU, the eyes are usually placed about one-third in from the edge of the frame, but this depends on any gestures the subject may make.

LS
Long shot
¾ profile

MLS
Medium long shot
¾ profile

MS
Medium shot
¾ profile

87

The position of the eyes on the vertical axis is based on the one-third convention. That is, if the vertical area is divided equally into three, then the eyes lie somewhere around two-thirds up from the lower edge of the frame. Whilst being a general guideline, the exact measurement is dependent upon the headroom for that subject and is relative to any other subject's headroom in the same sequence.

The three-quarters profile is the most common of all objective shots of a single subject. Well framed, the shot will fulfil most audience requirements. Badly framed, it gives direction problems and leads to audience confusion.

MCU
Medium close-up
¾ profile

CU
Close-up
¾ profile

BCU
Big close-up
¾ profile

The profile

Profile shots are not common. They are rarely ever used in documentary shooting, except where unplanned action requires it. In most cases the profile is used in drama, where story information to the audience is to be restricted. It relates to the audience's need to see clearly the eyes of the subject. As soon as this is not possible, as in the profile, the audience's interpretation of the subject changes.

The shot is often used in sequences where secrecy, distrust or aloofness is to be suggested, or where there is a need to withold the subject from the audience in some way.

The position of the eye in the profile shot is not as critical as in the three-quarters profile, but the basic framing as applied to the direct to camera shots should be applied.

LS
Long shot
High angle
¾ profile

MCU
Medium close-up
High angle
¾ profile

CU
Close-up
High angle
¾ profile

MCU
Medium close-up
Low angle
¾ profile

CU
Close-up
Low angle
¾ profile

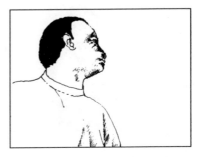

MCU
Medium close-up
Low angle
Profile

MCU
Medium close-up
High angle
Profile

CU
Close-up
High angle
Profile

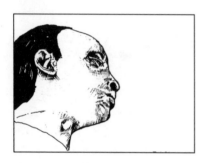

CU
Close-up
Low angle
Profile

MLS
Medium long shot
Profile

MS
Medium shot
Profile

MCU
Medium close-up
Profile

LS
Long shot
Low angle
Profile

MLS
Medium long shot
Low angle
Profile

MS
Medium shot
Low angle
¾ profile

CU
Close-up
Profile

BCU
Big close-up
Profile

The two shot

The two shot or 2S comprises two people in the frame. Such shots take one of three forms:

The profile two shot
The direct to camera two shot
The over shoulder two shot

In all cases, framing is of the highest importance. In addition, because one subject could be more important than the other, due to dialogue or action, then the framing may 'favour' one person more than the other. Favour is the emphasis placed on one subject, in a frame containing two or more subjects, by means of subject position, camera angle, lens angle or lighting.

The profile two shot
The most commom version of the profile two shot occurs in either the long shot or the medium long shot. In these framings there is enough room for action. When the shot is taken closer, as in the medium two shot, the subjects are standing so close together that the meaning of the shot changes to either argument or friendship. In the medium two shot there is only room for an action of the head. The closer the shot is framed, as in the close-up, the more it emphasises argument or friendship, to the extent that the action can eventually only be used in a scene depicting secrecy, anger or love.

The direct to camera two shot
The direct to camera version can be used up to the medium shot. To get closer than the MS, 'favour' must be used. This usually means arranging the subjects in juxtaposition (overlapping each other) with the lens focus either 'favouring' one or the other, or set in between the subjects to represent 'equal favour'. In setting the subjects in juxtaposition, care must be taken to attempt to match the subjects' heads relative to size and position in the frame.

Shots closer than the CU are not usually acceptable, as the juxtaposition becomes so great, in order to have both heads in frame, that the result looks too contrived for a subjective shot.

Profile two shot in medium long shot framing. Commonly used when action is required that is of normal speed.

Profile two shot in medium shot framing. Obviously used when subject action is above the waist.

In the medium close-up framing the two shot profile brings the subjects closer together. It begins to imply either confrontation or embrace.

The profile two shot in big close-up framing. The subjects are now so close together that the meaning to the audience is either secrecy, love or anger.

Direct two shot to camera. Framed as a medium the shot only allows for action above the waist. With people of differing heights, headroom can become a problem.

Direct two shot to camera. Here juxtaposition is used to squeeze the two subjects in the frame. The differing head heights, however, are now emphasised so that the subject on the left looks shorter; also the head sizes are too dissimilar to be convincing.

If the subject position is reversed, the head sizes are more similar, the headroom is similar and the emphasis is equal in 'favour'. This is a two shot direct to camera with close-up framing.

The over shoulder two shot

The most common of the two shots, this version is also the most adaptable, in that it has a natural 'favour'. For the audience, this means that attention can be given to one subject rather than dividing attention between two, as in the direct to camera version. The over shoulder is an objective shot. It edits well with the profile two shot.

In versions ranging from long shot to medium shot, either or both of the subjects have room for action and have sufficient space for a subject to move into or out of frame.

The most common version of the over shoulder is the medium close-up. Attention to the subject in 'favour' is clear, the position of both subjects in the frame is adaptable and the head sizes can be more easily matched.

Shots closer than the medium close-up however, bring particular problems. Once the shoulder of the subject closest to the camera disappears from frame, then the more the head is cut by the edge of the frame. The audience's attention, which should be aware of two people but devoted to one, is totally drawn to the subject in favour, but is also aware of an irritating out of focus shape on one side of the screen. The result is no longer an over shoulder and the shot would be better served by shooting a standard three-quarters profile of a single subject.

The long shot version of the over shoulder shot has ample room for movement.

There is also space in the medium shot framing to have variations in position of one of the subjects. Here the subject on the left is moving into the over shoulder position.

The standard over shoulder shot. The head sizes are similar as is the headroom. The distance between the two subjects seems to be normal, even though they are in reality standing quite close together.

In this example the over shoulder begins to become *un*acceptable. The heads are now badly framed and are cut by three sides of the frame.

This shot has ceased to become an over shoulder and would be better if the person on the left, now out of focus, were to be omitted completely.

97

Complex shots

Pans and tilts

Definitions

Horizontal
A pan is a pivotal movement of the camera and lens on a horizontal plane either from left to right or right to left. It may include a lens manipulation (focal length, focus or aperture) and should include a subject movement.

Vertical
A tilt is a pivotal movement of the camera and lens on the vertical plane either from low to high or the opposite way round. The tilt may also include a lens manipulation and should include a subject movement.

Diagonal
A pan and tilt is a combination of both horizontal and vertical plane movements which may include a lens manipulation and should include a subject movement.

General introduction

Without a moving subject, neither the pan nor the tilt resemble a natural physical eye movement. Our eyes neither pan nor tilt, but jump from spot to spot. If the eyes attempt to pan smoothly over a wall that happens to have things hanging on it, the opposite of the pan happens: the eyes take quick single images of the objects or points of interest and then scan or move fast to the next point of interest and repeat the process. The images are passed to the brain, and there the 'gaps' are filled in by reasoning. The eyes and the brain do this thousands of times each second. The brain then assembles the entire movement into what we call a pan.

The camera, in contrast to our eyes and mind, is a primitive instrument. It is a sign of a skilled cameraman that he can make the pan or tilt in such a way that it seems natural, and that the audience believes what it is seeing. Also, the audience belief in the movement is strengthened the more the subject of the pan or tilt is predominant.

PAN

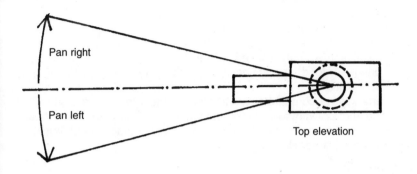

Pan right

Pan left

Top elevation

TILT

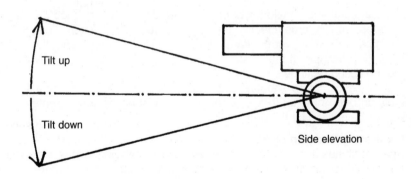

Tilt up

Tilt down

Side elevation

Practical considerations

The pan or tilt has to camouflage the unnatural element of swivelling our eyes, the solution to which lies in the foreground. The pan and tilt, like any other shot, should be made with depth. It should have at least backgrounds and foregrounds, and, preferably, middlegrounds. Whilst it is true that, physically, the eye jumps from spot to spot when trying to follow a background, it seems to be less so when following a foreground.

The reason for this lies in our early history of man the hunter. A hunter's eyes or ears immediately focused on movement, because movement could mean danger or food. Application of this human trait is the key to successful pans and tilts.

By arranging a comparatively strong movement in the foreground, the eyes and ears are immediately drawn to that and never to the background. So, the more the attention is drawn to the foreground movement, the more believable the pan or tilt seems to be.

Shooting the pan or tilt

Pan or tilt should be shot, normally, by following an action in the foreground. The pan or tilt depends on the shot framing and a great deal on the background. The strength of the action depends on the extent to which the background is in focus or not.

A pan or tilt made with a strong moving action in the foreground with an out of focus background can be very effective, but may seem a little unnatural or detached. A pan or tilt shot without any foreground movement is very unnatural and should never be considered without very good reason.

For pan or tilts to be effective they have to be well motivated. The motivation can take many forms. If the motivation is in the foreground, the pan is hardly noticeable. If the action is in the background, then the motivation and the action must be stronger.

In all cases, when shooting either a pan or tilt, the general practices apply and, for the shot to appear natural, it must never draw attention to itself or be noticed by the audience.

The parts of the pan or tilt

A pan or tilt has a number of component parts. Each part is critical and to omit any is to pass fundamental problems to the editor. The parts are:

- The start frame.
- The camera and lens movement.
- The end frame.

The start frame

The start frame is the shot within which the action or movement will begin. The start frame must be in existence for some seconds prior to the action and is framed as a simple shot. Therefore, the camera must be completely static. The start frame is the frame into which the editor will cut from the shot which goes before. Consequently, the start frame should have no

Panning a scene from A to B is not natural.

Never pan just to get there. If there is no foreground action, use two or more separate shots to get there.

Panning with a moving foreground is natural …

or following an action.

other strong movements in the background which will distract the audience from the subject or object movement in the foreground.

The camera movement
The camera movement is that, either horizontally, vertically or both together, which follows the start frame and continues without interruption to the end frame. The subject movement is framed as a simple shot and contains sufficient space on the side of the frame towards which the subject or action is directed or moving.

If this part of the Pan or Tilt were frozen for examination at any single point, the result should resemble a well composed simple shot. Consequently, perfect framing throughout the camera movement is a prerequisite of this part of the shot. To overcome the possibility of the start of the camera movement being 'noticed' by the audience, it is synchronised to the subject movement, so that the audience's attention is drawn to the action on screen and to nothing else.

The camera movement should end before the subject movement. This will automatically be achieved if the 'looking space', 'nose room' or 'looking room' (the space in the screen which leads the movement) was correctly preserved during the camera movement, and will lead naturally to the end frame.

THE PAN (OR TILT)

The start frame	The pan	The end frame

Start   Pan   End

103

The end frame

The end frame is the part in which the subject action or movement will end. It should remain for some seconds after the camera movement and is framed as a simple shot. Therefore, like the start frame, it must be a completely static camera, without any 'drift'. Drift or drifting is small but unwanted movement of the pan and tilt head at the beginning or at the end of a shot.

The end frame is the frame into which the editor will cut out of, from the pan or tilt, into the next shot or sequence. There should be no great noticeable background movement after the subject action has been completed which might distract the audience.

These three parts, when carried out smoothly together, and with the correct, motivated, action will result in a pan or a tilt that is virtually unnoticeable by the audience.

Unorthodox pans and tilts

It is possible to pan or tilt without a foreground or background subject action. This is mostly carried out when:

(a) there is a motivation to begin the pan;
(b) when the pan is so slow that the camera movement is not noticed by the audience and
(c) when the shot is subjective.

In some cases, often in news coverage, a pan or tilt is used in conjunction with a lens movement. This is normally an attempt to camouflage the zoom. Without a strong motivation, however, this typical news shot is only rarely satisfactory.

There are hardly any circumstances when a pan or tilt, used only to go from one place to another, is ever justified.

START FRAME

No movement of camera.

No strong movements, other than the main action.

No activity in background which will distract.

PAN

Movement of camera synchronized with action.

Camera leads action.

More space at A.

Less space at B.

END FRAME

Camera movement ends before subject.

No great background movement.

105

Other movements in the complex shot

Focus

Focus is the position in which an object or subject is situated, so that the image produced by the lens is well defined. If the image is well defined it is said to be 'sharp' i.e. totally in focus. If the image is totally undefined it is called OOF i.e. out of focus. If the image is only slightly undefined, the focus is called 'soft'.

The operation of adjusting focus from one subject to another is called either 'throwing focus' or 'pulling focus'. Throwing focus is moving the focus position from a subject in the foreground to another subject in the background. Pulling focus is the opposite way round, i.e. focusing closer to the camera.

The focusing range available, from furthest to closest, depends on the lens angle. A wide lens angle, 40 degrees and over, has nearly no possibilities for focus movement, but a narrow lens angle, less than 20 degrees, has many possibilities of focus movement from foreground to background.

Shifting focus from foreground to background (or the opposite way around) is something our eyes and brain do quite naturally. The brain selects where it wants the focus to be generally because of a motivation, either in words or movement. The cameraman ideally uses a motivation in order to pull or throw focus, so that the lens focus movement will not be noticed by the audience.

Zoom

The zoom is an infinite set of lenses. The action of going from one lens angle (focal length) to another is called zooming, which, in complete contrast to throwing focus, is a highly artificial movement. Zooming does not resemble any natural eye or brain movement. Consequently, it differs from other movements in the complex shot in that it cannot be seen on its own.

Changing the framing by use of the zoom should only be done in the complex shot when the movement of the zoom is hidden by movement of either the subject, camera, focus or a combination of all three.

Focus sharp on foreground

'Throw focus' to the background

MLS framing

A zoom to MCU gives *no* change in perspective

Combining the movements

The complex shot is made up of the combined movements of subject, lens and camera. The number of combinations are many and range from a pan of a subject walking, to a more intricate complex shot of a pan and tilt of subjects with a focus pull and zoom.

There are three common factors to all complex shots.

1 It is the subject action that determines the movement
The action of the subject begins and ends the movement of both the lens and camera.

Example
A subject is walking from background to foreground and turns to exit screen left. The shot begins with a (LA) low angle long shot, tilting down at the same time to maintain headroom, and as the subject approaches the foreground begins to pan left. The final framing is reached before the pan ends.

In this case, it is the action of the man walking into the foreground that forces the tilt and zoom. It is the turn to the left that instigates the pan.

2 All movements must be combined
Movements must be fluid and must overlap each other, unless there is a break in the action. The amount of overlap depends on the subject action. In the case above, the tilt should begin before the zoom, so that the attention of the audience is drawn to the movement of the subject rather than the zoom.

In nearly all shots, a zoom should never come first, it should be preceded by a camera movement.

3 On the 'still', a complex shot should resemble a simple shot
If, at any point during the complex shot, the picture were to be stilled or frozen, then the resultant framing should resemble a simple shot.

Low angle
From the LS the
tilt begins as the
zoom works the
reframe

The man turns
screen left and
this motivates the
pan

The pan in the
MS

The pan is
completed before
the subject exits
frame

109

Developing shots

The developing shot is the same as the complex one, but with yet one more additional movement, that of the camera support. The movement can be in one of three axes or even a combination of axes:

Track, in or out.
Crab, right or left.
Elevate, up or depress, down.

Combining all the other movements of subject or subjects, lens focus, framing (zoom), pans and tilts, with a movement of a camera support, into one fluid movement, makes for a very complicated shot. It is difficult and often expensive to make, and is unlikely to be the work of a beginner. It is impossible to be carried out by one person. In most developing shots the support will be moved by two people (grips), another person will be framing (camera operator) and another (assistant cameraman) will be carrying out lens adjustments.

Some developing shots, made up of only three movements, e.g. a track, pan and subject movement, can be made in a much simpler way, but still need additional manpower.

The three factors combining movement in the developing shot are the same as those in the complex shot:

1. The subject action determines the movement.
2. The movements must be combined.
3. If stilled, the result should resemble a simple shot.

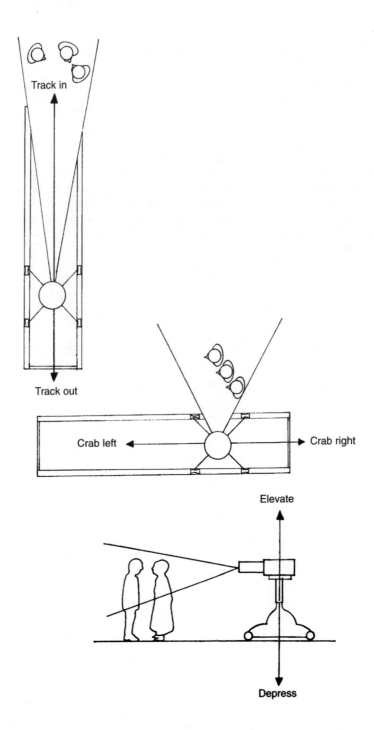

Track in

Track out

Crab left

Crab right

Elevate

Depress

General practices

Introduction

General practices should be regarded as binding. They are not only professionally required, but often contractually. Most general practices are based on good common sense, professional history of the craft and an extensive knowledge of what is fair and reasonable and what is not.

As with other craft skills involved in the practice of picture making, e.g. editing and sound, the creative process is very important. Unlike the Arts, where creativity can exist without technique, shooting pictures must have a technical process in order to exist. But this does not preclude creativity. 'Creativity overrules grammar' is as true in shooting as in any other craft skills.

The general practices are as follows:

- The reason for shooting is editing.
- Show the audience what they need to see.
- Never be obtrusive.
- Know your equipment.
- Know your subject.
- Know your sun.
- Motivate each shot.
- Pass solutions to the editor, never problems.

Explanation of the general practices

The reason for shooting is editing

This practice is probably the most important and has become so as the role of post-production editing becomes stronger. In the early days, producers and directors had a saying: 'If you can't cut it, don't shoot it.' This was because they understood that if a better story could be had with pictures from differing viewpoints, and the better those viewpoints fitted together, then the more convincing the story seemed to be.

When shooting any activity, documentary or drama it is important to recognise and understand the process which presents that activity to the public. Taking the process for a documentary as an example.

Pre-production: SELECTED REALITY
An activity which is observed in real or actual time, using five human senses.

Production: TAKE REALITY APART
Shooting selected fragments of the reality using two senses only (sight and sound).

Post-production (1): REASSEMBLE REALITY
Reassembly of the shot fragments into a rough cut or test story. This gives a new story, 'our' story, with a new duration.

Post-production (2): NEW VERSION OF REALITY
Using post-production techniques and a visual 'language', a new version of the reality is made. The truth of the reality has been reinvented to fit duration, audience expectation, station or producer's policy etc. Completed in two senses.

Viewing: REINVENTION ESTABLISHED
The viewers now watch an idealised form of what was experienced in the beginning. It has to be understood with fewer senses, in a different time, with less experiences, and with less environmental and geographical knowledge than the original.

Show the audience what they need to see

When shooting for directors, the choice of shots is usually made by them, but in shooting documentary, magazine or news, the decision of what to shoot is often made by the cameraman. In this case, the cameraman should always be aware of what the audience needs to see.

The audience has an expectation and denying that expectation makes for mental frustration. Every action on the screen requires a corresponding 're-action'. It is often the 're-action' shot that explains the action. If the audience see a man looking at something, then they also want to see what the man is looking at. They need to see it in order to satisfy their own curiosity. Not to include the re-action shot (what the man is looking at) works in drama, where denial of visual information assists the plot. But, to deny information in a programme which sets out to be a document of events is a mistake.

For example, in a programme about guitar music, a guitarist is talking about fingering and then demonstrates what she is talking about. It would be unthinkable if the shot of the hand on the guitar neck were not shown. The audience want to see it and need to see it, in order to understand what the musician is talking about.

The cameramen should never deny the audience information which is vital to their understanding of the story or scene.

If a musician is talking about fingering

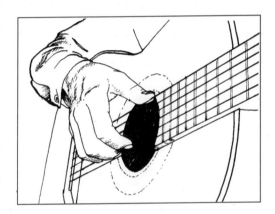

and makes a demonstration

the audience *need* to see what is being demonstrated.

117

Never be obtrusive

The cameraman should never shoot a shot that appears obtrusive. Put another way, no shot should ever be more noticeable than the action or activity it is showing. Very skilled cameramen claim that a shot that is 'seen' by the audience as being 'unpleasantly noticeable' is, consequently, a bad shot.

Obtrusive camera work draws attention to itself and away from the action. In post-production, the editing stage, obtrusive camera work seems to become emphasised and this overemphasis presents itself to the audience as a distraction. The main reason for this is, that whilst the shot may seem exciting, an element of the audience's attention, however small, is drawn away from the action to the technique of the shot. The result is that some 'viewing reality' is lost.

A cameraman must be always observant, but never obtrusive.

A shot which changes from the LS

into an obtrusive view.

Either there is an earthquake, or it is an effect.

119

Know your equipment

Of all the equipment a cameraman might use; camera, batteries, mounts, heads etc., the camera lens is probably the most important. The lens is the camera's eye. Like human eyes, they vary from type to type. But there are principles. Without knowing these principles and how to use them the cameraman is guessing. Whilst guessing is allowed in some professions, in programme making it is not. The money spent in shooting invariably belongs to someone else so it is a matter of professional pride that the cameramen should be aware of their equipment and its limitations.

It is not important for a beginner to know the scientific formulae for corrective lenses and how to calculate them, but it is very important to know how good the lens is, and the extent to which a cameraman can trust it. It is critical to know the relationship between F stops, focal lengths/lens angle, focus differences and filters, and how these relationships can be used.

Many of the essential requirements for the cinematographer are not applicable to the electronic cameraman, but there are similarities. For knowledge of stock, in film work, one should substitute magnetic tape, when working electronically, for lenses; there is no substitute for knowledge.

There have been many volumes written on lenses, ranging from books for beginners to David Samuelson's 'Hands on Manual for Cinematographers', and beginners should be urged to make the subject a special study.

Know your subject

It is a highly skilled and daring documentary cameraman that is prepared to shoot a situation without knowing what is likely to happen. Most cameramen prefer not to try improvisation, unless there are no alternatives. This is not because cameramen believe that an improvised shot won't work, but because it might have too much risk or luck involved. Cameramen have a saying: 'A good shot may have a lucky element, but not the opposite way around.' Good shots are worked out beforehand and the better the cameraman knows the subject, the better the shots. To do this there is no substitute for looking.

In documentary shooting, for example, if a man is to be shown walking his daily route to work, it is important for the cameraman to watch the man do it before the shooting. Only then will it become obvious what to shoot, where to place the camera, what backgrounds and foregrounds are important, and which actions are vital to show. Also, by watching the action beforehand, it will be possible to tell how the entire duration of the walk can be reduced to the recorded fragments which will reasonably simulate the walk in the 'film time' allowed for the sequence.

Without forehand knowledge, even the simplest shooting operation is liable to complications. Complications cause uncertainties and may give variable results. Knowing the subject to be shot is a highly important part of the cameraman's work.

Know your light

Light comes from two sources, natural and artificial. Natural light comes from the sun and most shooting uses natural light as much as possible. Consequently, knowing the position of the sun when shooting is another important element in the work of the cameraman.

The sun moves at such a fixed time that people used to set clocks by it. So light relates to time. The sun travels 180 degrees from sunrise to sunset and it does this in 12 hours, 15 degrees each hour. But, 15 degrees measured in distance at ground or camera level is many metres. So a shot set up to show a particular shadow must be either lit artificially, or carefully set up prior to that time. Mistakes in calculating where the sun will be, make for expensive retakes the following day.

Depending how far the location is from the equator also poses other problems. In some countries where the midday sun lies almost directly overhead, then the shadow is very short as compared to very long shadows at sunset. Where the sun is very high, the problem of unwanted shadows, especially on the face of a subject, becomes more acute, and extensive use of various types of sun reflection equipment becomes a major activity. In addition, in some parts of the world, the actual usable shooting time in any day is significantly reduced because of the power of the sun. Nevertheless, the usable sun must be calculated and used for the best results. In Northern and Central Europe, the light can be more filtered and less severe than the dry season in India, Sri Lanka or Central Africa.

For the cameraman, the short period when the sun has disappeared below the horizon or alternatively, just before sunrise, known as the 'golden time' or 'golden minutes', is probably the most rewarding because of the soft, rich quality of the natural light. But, as the name suggests, the working time is very short during this period and significant planning is required to make full use of it.

The sun in camerawork can be either an enemy or a friend. Once a cameraman understands where it will be, and for how long, techniques can be learnt to use it.

Motivate each shot

There are two good reasons why each shot should be motivated:

- It makes for a more interesting shot.
- It gives the post-production editor an increased choice of cutting points.

The motivation should be 'built in' either in the vision or in the sound.

For example, a shot of a garden or a park need not only contain the garden. Something should happen which will help to explain to the audience what the nature of the garden or park is. Often things happen to explain its location. A woman pushing a pram through the shot with heavy traffic sounds in the background will explain to the audience that the park is in the centre of a town. Low-flying aircraft will mean that it is near to a busy airport. If the woman pushing the pram is wearing a uniform of a 'nanny' it means that the park is in the more wealthy part of town. If the trees are big and old then it is a long-standing park. The trees and flowers will tell the audience what season it is. Birds and animals will tell more.

Often many of these visual or aural motivations will act as clues and will give the audience information which will explain the shot to a greater extent than the shot without motivations.

For example, an empty street is not just an empty street. It should have something that makes it look empty and gives it meaning. The famous New York shot very early morning would not be the same without the steam coming from the road grating in the foreground. The shot needs the lorry (truck) rumbling past through the water left by the night's rain. In the shot is encapsulated all the elements of what makes a street in that city at that time.

If, in shooting documentary, a motivation is not there, it does not mean to say that it could not be there; for example, shooting a bear in a zoo with its keeper, rather than without.

Often the motivations have to be created or invented, but something or someone will exist which can be put into the shot which makes the shot more real, giving it more meaning for the audience.

122

Pass solutions to the editor, never problems

The entire purpose of the cameraman's shots is that they can be passed to the next process of the manufacture of the programme. The next process is editing. A good cameraman will know something about it, so that he is aware, especially when shooting, of the requirements of the editor. Consequently, each shot should contain the elements needed for the editor to make the transition from one shot to another, even if the final order of shots is not known at the time of shooting.

Solutions, therefore, refer to editing solutions; that is, a shot which has a number of possible editing points. In other words, a shot which can be edited in a number of ways.

If the shot contains all the elements, it is likely that it will edit easily. The less elements the shot has, the less likely it will be to edit. Shots without any elements make serious problems for the editor. Knowingly passing bad shots to the editor and expecting the shooting problems to be solved is a bad practice.

Overlapping action and shooting ratio

Overlapping action

An 'action', as a noun, is the name given to any subject(s) movement or activity. As a verb, it is used to begin the movement or activity of the subject(s). Overlapping action refers to the noun.

For an editor to cut two shots together with continuity (an action edit or continuity edit), both shots must have sufficient action so that the selected editing point is available on both. To do this the cameraman shoots extra parts of the action at the beginning and at the end of the shot so that the editor can more accurately join the shots together. It will then appear that none of the complete action is lost. These extra parts of the action are called 'overlapping action'.

The amount of overlapping action varies according to the shot and the action. Some actions are short and require only a second, some require many seconds. Generally, the closer the shot the less overlapping action is required, and the wider, the more.

Example
A scene calls for a standing subject to leave a room through a door to a corridor outside the room. Shooting with a single camera, the scene has to be divided into two shots: one, the subject leaving the room; and two, the subject entering and walking down the corridor.

If the action is to appear natural, then the appearance of the subject going through the door, from one space to another, should not be interrupted by looking as if it were two different shots, or the illusion is lost. Consequently, the action is done twice; once seen from the inside and once seen from the corridor.

The action from the inside should be up to and including the closing of the door as the subject has passed through it. The action from the outside must be from the closed door with the subject on the inside, who then opens the door, walks through it, and exits down the corridor.

The overlapping action is that which involves the door, because it is within that part that the editor will attempt to find the continuity, identical in both shots, within which will be at least one frame where the cut can be made.

The reasons for the overlapping action are:

1. To allow maximum choice for the editor to select the cutting point.
2. To allow time for the subject to reproduce the action more fluently.

SHOT 1
Inside the room

Subject approaches the door.

Subject opens the door

goes through the door

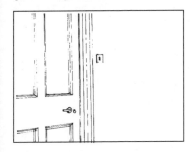

and closes the door.

SHOT 2
Outside, in the corridor

Begin with the closed door.

Subject (on the inside) opens the door

comes through the door

closes the door and exits screen.

125

Problems in shooting overlapping action

1. Matching the speed of action.
2. Continuity.
3. Overshooting.

1. Matching the speed of action

The apparent speed of an action depends on the framing of the shot. Even though the actual speed of the action by the subject is exactly the same, it will appear different and may give a problem when cutting the shot to another. For example, on a long shot the action of a person will seem slightly slower than the same action on, say, a close-up. This is because the movement seen on the screen on a long shot is less than the movement seen on a close-up of the same action.

Example

A subject picks up a glass from a table and drinks from it. If a close-up of the glass and hand, seen picking it up, is needed, then overlapping action will have to be shot. The shot would start with the hand out of the frame, the hand comes into frame and picks up the glass, then the hand and the glass exit frame.

On examination it will be seen that the distance of the movement of the hand on the long shot is significantly more than that on the close-up. But, as the action is the same, it will appear to the audience that the hand has moved faster on the close-up.

This might be overcome if a third shot, drinking from the glass, were used. Then, overlapping action would require the glass to be picked up again, even though the shot might be only shooting a medium close-up of the subject.

Solution

Besides taking the close-up at normal action speed, two other takes should be made of a slightly slower action. The editor can then select the one which seems to match the long shot better.

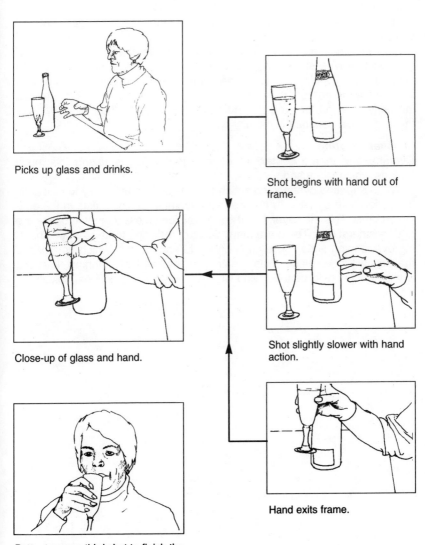

Picks up glass and drinks.

Shot begins with hand out of frame.

Close-up of glass and hand.

Shot slightly slower with hand action.

Hand exits frame.

Better to use a third shot to finish the sequence.

2 Continuity

Continuity is the exact matching of the detail of subjects, objects and situations from take to take. In overlapping action this also includes light and sound.

Most problems are concerned with people rather than objects. In shooting documentary, especially, it is unrealistic to ask a guest to repeat an action for overlapping in exactly the same way as the previous take. This is because the person, the subject, is more likely to carry out their actions instinctively. Therefore, the cameraman in documentary has to be aware of this and make constant continuity checks.

3 Overshooting

Overshooting in the context of overlapping action is taking too much footage which is unused.

When shooting overlapping action there is often a tendency to repeat all the action take by take, to ensure that maximum choice exists in the editing process. This, however, is not good practice unless money and time are not considerations. There are many ways of reducing footage when shooting overlapping action. The main one is to know within which boundaries the edit will take place. This requires an element of planning, knowing which shots should be taken and why. A story-board is an ideal solution.

Shooting ratio

Shooting ratio is the relationship of footage shot to that used, and is expressed as a ratio where footage used is taken as unity. Thus, shooting 10:1 means that ten times the footage that was actually needed was shot. Shooting ratio is used by the producer as a formula to help calculate the cost of a production.

There is no standard figure, no benchmark, which a beginner can apply; it depends on the type of shoot. For example, shooting wildlife is very expensive in footage; 60:1 is not uncommon. On the other hand, scenes with predictable machine movement can be as low as 5:1.

Shooting ratio can also be expressed in time. For example, if an interview is to last, when edited, 5 minutes in length, and one 20 minute cassette is used, then the ratio is 4:1.

Even if the shot is managed in one take, it does not mean that the footage shot is the footage used. This is because the entire take is made up of pieces of footage which are important to the process of manufacture, of which only one part is the action itself. Thus the minimum ratio for even a perfect take is 2:1.

In drama shooting, 2:1 is not a reasonable possibility. The ratio usually depends on the complexity of the shot. Simple shots have a smaller ratio, while complex and developing shots have a larger one.

Shooting drama on magnetic tape at a higher ratio has other implications. If the finished programme is to last 60 minutes, and the ratio is 20:1, then the amount of tape used is some 20 hours. This is a considerable amount of footage to process and results in added expenditure in the post-production stage.

It is, therefore, a question of experience and negotiation as to the ratio the novice cameraman can expect.

Working practices

Introduction

The working practices are guides for the daily practice of shooting. The practices have been found to work mainly because of years of shooting from reputable cameramen around the world finding solutions to everyday problems. Working practices change because of fashion and new technology, but do not change because of viewing habits. Sometimes a shot will not work, or it works on location but not in the editing room. This is because shooting is not a science; neither is it an art form, though it can sometimes come close to it. It is at its best an imperfect craft, where the predictable can be in direct opposition to the unpredictable.

Shooting in locations which can be hostile produces additional working practices, as does wildlife photography. Indeed, almost any location and any circumstance can generate its own practices. But there are common factors, which, applied with common sense, will benefit the beginner. It is those working practices which follow.

Never shoot movement on a BCU

Reasons

The big close-up is the closest shot of the face without being a detail. The face covers 100% of the screen and, therefore, movement, for example of the eyes, also covers a large area of the screen. If an editor attempts a continuity cut to a wider shot of the same person, the difference in the continuity, either in size or position, is so great that the edit jumps.

Any movement of the subject made on close shots is magnified so greatly that it can become over-exaggerated and theatrical. The BCU magnifies most of all; so movement, even the slightest nod or eye flicker, takes on another meaning because of its size.

Solutions

Subject movement should not be attempted in drama without a very experienced subject who has the ability to suggest a facial movement without seeming to make it. For example, in a love scene where a kiss has to be shown, movement of the lips must be very small to appear to be romantic or the result can be something else.

The BCU should be very rarely used as it is often very difficult to edit.

Exceptions

The exceptions to the practice are when the BCU is shot with a very wide lens angle in order to enhance distortion, as in some horror sequences which require bizarre effects. Another exception might be in a dramatic fight scene where movement can be so fast that it can add to the overall impact of the sequence.

Also, exceptions are sometimes possible in documentaries where the BCU is held for longer on screen, giving the audience more time to become accustomed to the unusual scale of the face. In this situation, however, the story of the subject has to be strong enough to engage the audience more than the scale.

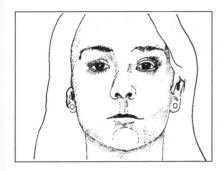

A movement of as little as 2 cm

will put the subject out of frame
or even out of focus.

A smile on a medium close-up

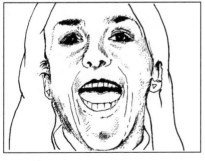

becomes strange on a CU.

Use discretion in the use of the CU

Reasons
The close-up, CU, has a very specific meaning. The audience's attention is drawn to the face so completely that it precludes all other information and concentrates only on facial characteristics. Whilst this can be expressive, it can also be too revealing. Skin tones, blemishes, hairs and wrinkles take on extraordinary proportions and, as in the BCU, the movement of an eyelid, nose or lips can appear to be quite considerable as all movement is magnified.

Solutions
The use of the CU and the BCU should be reserved for scenes where the natural position of a viewer would be at a similar distance from the subject and this size of a face might be seen. Some of these situations are as follows.

Love scenes, where the apparent size of the CU would represent the closeness of one of two people face to face, standing, sitting or lying.

Aggression, often shown in full profile in order to get two faces, framed nose to nose. In a single person shot, the CU is often a subjective shot.

Examination, where one person could be examining a particular part of another's face or their own, e.g. a doctor examining a patient's face or a dentist examining a mouth. In self-examination, a man examining his chin before a morning shave or a woman putting on make-up using a mirror.

Secrets, where it is necessary to show that the information is secret from everyone, except the audience. Usually shown either as one full face and one profile or by two overlapping profiles. Whichever is used, the mouth of one person will be touching the ear of another.

Loss of framing or focus must be overcome by reducing subject movement. Depth of field problems are sometimes evident.

Exceptions
The main exception to this practice is usually in 'hot news' sequences, e.g. the CU of the disaster victim. Another is during bizarre sequences in TV advertisements or in special effects.

134

USE OF THE CU

Love scene where the distance from the subject is in relation to that which it might be in real life.

Or, in aggresion.

Or, when telling a secret.

On MCU and closer, don't forget the eyes

Reasons
It is one of the factors of human life that health, beauty and even attentiveness is often reflected in the state of a subject's eyes. This is very true in shooting. A subject's eyes can seem normal in the MLS, but closer, with the MCU and CU, the eyes are bigger on screen and can appear flat and lifeless and seem to lose their sparkle, even though the shot is perfectly in focus.

Solutions
The solution is to replace the sparkle with an artificial highlight from either a reflector, or from small lighting units (often called inkie dinkies), correctly placed. In both cases, using reflector or artificial lighting, the equipment should be at the appropriate height which would resemble where a light source might have been.

The aim would be to get one white spot in each eyeball of the subject. The white spot in the eyeball will be the shape of the light source. This is very common in unlit interiors where, if the subject is facing the window, the white spot is a reflection of the rectangle of a window. Therefore, the replacement white spot should follow that shape.

Exterior light sources for highlighting can take various forms but the main one is the sun. Consequently, the position of the reflector must attempt to copy this by never being lower than the subject's eyes.

Exceptions
Where the subject's eyes need, for dramatic purposes, to be flat, then highlights must be removed.

Infinite distance light or Inkie Dinkie.

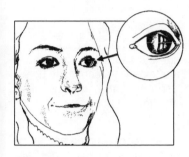

This could be a reflection from window or light source.

For an exterior shot, light should be reflected this way (above the eye level).

Never this way.

At sunset a reflector can be placed at normal eye level, but the sun never goes below it.

When shooting the unplanned, unscripted pan, shoot both directions

Reasons
This mainly applies to documentary shooting and is concerned with editing decisions as to how the pan is used. Often the preceding shot could follow a subject having a different screen direction and, consequently, the shots will not cut convincingly.

Solutions
Shoot the pan with the subject going both directions, once screen left to right and once screen right to left. This way the editor can make the direction fit.

Example
A woman is walking to work. It is required that she is seen walking directly to work without changes in direction, which might not be the case in reality. If the nature of the shooting is intermittent and shot over an extended period of time, it is quite possible that, without extensive continuity notes, the screen direction can be mistaken. Shooting the pan both ways gives the editor a chance to overcome this problem should it occur.

Exceptions
Where there are continuity notes available, or in highly scripted and storyboarded shooting scripts, as in drama productions (see section on Pans and tilts).

A subject is walking right.

If the previous shot is followed by this shot, then the two shots together mean the subject has changed direction.

But this is not so if the direction is the same.

Keep individual action away from the edge of the frame

Reason
Action, when on the edge of the frame, may be disturbed by domestic cut-off, especially in the LS and wider shots.

Solutions
Reframe during the shot if shooting a documentary or, in a prescripted shot, rearrange the action.

Exceptions
The main exception to this practice is where the subject actually leaves the frame in preparation for the editor to cut to another shot. In this case, the composition of the shot just prior to the subject leaving is critical, because the audience's attention is drawn from the subject to the remaining background.

Another exception to the practice is during a fast action scene, where the subject may go near the frame edge but the action continues and the subject returns more centre-frame.

Keep the action in the frame.

Reframe the shot if required.

Frame the subject and object on opposite sides of the frame when shooting for a directional edit

Reason
If two people are looking at each other or a person is looking at something, they leave their own natural space between themselves and the object or subject. When this natural space is divided into two shots, one of the person who is looking and the other of that which is being looked at, then the natural space is equally divided into two parts, one part per shot, the space being composed in the opposite side of the frame to the other shot.

Solutions
Say a woman is looking at a building. There will be a natural place where she will stand in order to see the building or part of it. This is the position she feels comfortable with. If the picture is in two shots, then if the woman is shot screen left, the building will be shot screen right. This simulates, to the audience, that if the two pictures were joined together, the space is in between the woman and the building. If the two spaces are on the same side of the screen then, when edited together, the result is disturbing and unconvincing, mainly because it looks as if the figure is fighting the frame.

Exceptions
When shooting for directional edits, there are no exceptions to this practice.

142

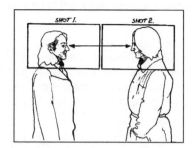

This is a natural space.

Shot 1

Shot 2

It is the same for a building.

If the natural looking space is removed the sequence is not so convincing.

When shooting a dialogue, check the matching shot first

Reason
The matching shot, sometimes called the reverse angle shot, is the shot which is usually made after the master shot and is the mirror opposite. Often the temptation to shoot an unplanned master shot has the result that the position and camera angle for the matching shot is forgotten at the time. The result is that, when the matching shot is called for:

(a) it will not fit into the environment; or
(b) there are major spurious objects in the background; or
(c) there is an eye line problem between the two subjects; or
(d) there are depth of field problems.

Solutions
The fundamental reason for the mistakes happening is that the location was not checked correctly before the master shot was taken. If there is likely to be a problem, a little plan should be drawn up to help in deciding where the master and the matching shots should be.

It might be discovered at this stage that there is physically no space to shoot a matching shot, and consequently the master shot can be changed into something more suited to the environment.

Exceptions
The exceptions to this practice are mainly in news work, where the speed of the shooting is often the cause for not being able to carry out matching shots.

a)

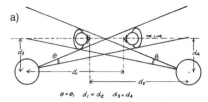

$\theta = \theta_1 \quad d_1 = d_2 \quad d_3 = d_4$

A matching shot is that which matches another in camera angle, lens angle and distance from the subject.

b)

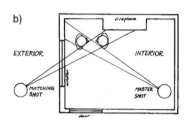

In this example, the master shot is possible, but there is no space to shoot the matching interior shot, without using a wide angle which would give a different depth of field. The two shots would not edit smoothly, but the backgrounds would jump.

The exterior matching shot would be possible but should only be used at the beginning or end of the sequence if the action was moving from the exterior into the interior or from the interior into the exterior.

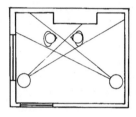

This would be better, but the corner of the room (unless the depth of field was small) would be evident.

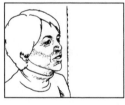

When these two shots are edited together the vertical line representing the corner of the room would jump.

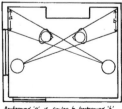

Background 'a' is similar to background 'b'

This would be an improvement, but now the light from the window would begin to have a predominant effect on the shot.

When shooting man-made objects, choose a framing which best uses the aspect ratio

Reason
The moment a framing is selected, then attention is drawn to what is inside the frame. And the more that it (that which is isolated) is related by closeness or juxtaposition to the edges of the frame, then the greater seems the impact of the image.

Solution
For objects which have a far greater length than width, there are two ways of overcoming the framing problem.

Method 1: Shoot the object with the less interesting part in the background and the more recognisable part in the foreground. The object should be placed or the camera positioned in such a way that the new perspective of the object fits within the aspect ratio.

Method 2: Take two shots of the object, a wide shot covering the entire object in its environment, and the second, a detail of the salient part of the object which describes its function.

Example 1
A train is travelling across the screen left to right. If the entire train is shot, it would stretch from the left-hand side frame edge to the right-hand side frame edge and would be so small that it might just resemble a line. The solution is to shoot the train travelling from background to foreground, i.e. shoot at an angle to the train, so that the train shape, when in the foreground, better fits the aspect ratio and the characteristics of a train.

Example 2
A flag-pole with flag flying. The solution here is to use two shots. The first would be a long shot of the flag on the flag-pole in relationship to the environment, and the second shot would be a detail of the top of the flag-pole with the flag attached and flying.

A train on an XLS screen moving from left to right will show direction and landscape.

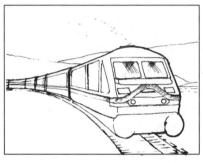

This shot more fulfils the aspect ratio, and also shows direction and movement. It can be used in conjunction with the XLS (above) or even on its own.

Showing clearly which flag is flying on the embassy flag-pole …

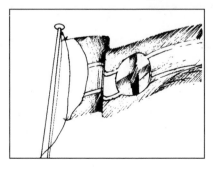

… needs a second shot.

Care should be taken with the two shot method in maintaining the position of the object from the first shot to the second. Thus, if the flag-pole is in the left-hand side of the screen in the first shot then, to avoid a jump when joining the two shots together, the pole should continue to be in the left-hand side in the second shot.

Exceptions
The exceptions to this working practice are:

(a) When the object is a minor part of the function, in which case the main function is shot first and then a series of closer shots which arrive at the detail required.
(b) Any object e.g. a child's hoop which is described only by its outer edge, and has an enclosed area which does not add to the shot unless the child is playing with it. In shooting the hoop alone, it would have to be tilted to gain the correct perspective.
(c) Any object which must be shown in its correct geometrical proportions, e.g. a round tyre, if tilted becomes an oval. This is important in ETV programmes.

Sometimes, in framing an object to the aspect ratio, it can take on unlikely proportions and cause puzzlement with the audience as to its identity. For example, a screwdriver shot in close-up, using method 1, is unlikely to indicate its function unless it is shown doing what it is designed to do or can be otherwise identified, for example by commentary.

Some objects might be so familiar to the audience that the function might not need to be explained even when the perspective is changed. But in most cases, if the function cannot be explained in one shot, then it should be in an additional shot.

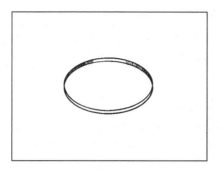

A child's circular hoop may not be instantly recognisable to the audience, because: a) the perspective has been adjusted to fit the aspect ratio; b) the shot is isolated from its function.

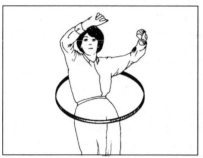

By including the function the child's hoop is better 'explained'.

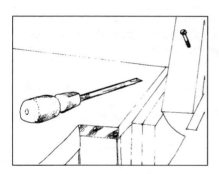

A screwdriver shot in close-up to fit the aspect ratio becomes an unfamiliar image.

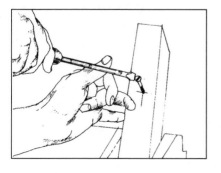

It needs a second shot to show its function.

When shooting matching shots of two people of differing heights, shoot dissimilar camera heights

Reason
The purpose is to overcome the dominant and submissive effects caused by apparently shooting low and high angles. If the camera takes the eye-line of a taller person, and holds the same camera height for the shorter person, then the effect is a shot which makes the shorter person look submissive. Also, in using the eyeline of the shorter person and using this camera height to shoot the taller person, the taller person is made to look even more dominant. It is important, where visual balance between two people is required, that camera heights are adjusted accordingly.

Solution
To gauge the camera heights required, the shot of the taller person (see diagram) looking slightly lower than eye level should match with the other shot of the shorter person looking slightly upwards. The method used is to project an imaginary line across the environment which also follows this eyeline between the two people. As one of the requirements of the matching shot is to have the distance from subject to camera the same in both shots, then the required camera height for the matching shot will lie on the projected line.

In some situations where the height difference is significant, this solution becomes impractical and the exceptions apply.

Exceptions
Where the height variation is such that differing camera heights cannot apply, other alternatives can be used.

1. Sit both subjects on chairs and use cushions to adjust the reduced difference in heights. Differing camera heights may still have to be used.
2. Raise the height of the shorter subject by using a box or rostra. Obviously, the box should not be shown on shot unless it is part of the story.
3. Place the taller of the subjects on a lower ground level.

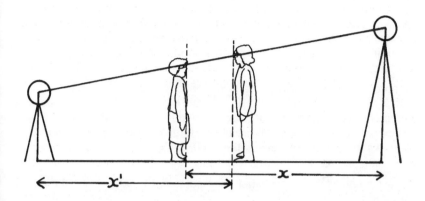

To obtain matching shots with subjects of differing heights, project the incline as shown. The shots will match when x^1 and x are similar, the lens angles are similar and the height of the camera lies on the incline. The shot is then taken down (or up) the incline.

Shoot constant headroom

Reasons

After a shot is made, it could be divided, during editing, into many smaller parts. This is a common practice during an interview, when the answers a guest gives to the questions put will be recorded as one single shot. If headroom is not constant, then, when edited, it will appear that the subject is either higher or lower in the frame each time a new part of the shot is used. In effect it looks as if the subject is bobbing up and down.

Solution

Headroom can be checked on a field monitor with a grid covering the monitor screen (see diagram). The grid can have various headrooms and screen divisions marked on it to accommodate different shots.

For example, if two people are talking to each other, then the headroom in both shots should be constant.

Exceptions

An exception to this rule is when the shot is such that it cannot be edited into parts; for example, the moving part of a subject in a pan or of a subject(s) in a developing shot.

Another exception is when there is a subject movement within a simple shot from say background to foreground, or in reverse, and it is shot without any lens movement.

This headroom is correct.

This headroom is too great.

If variations occur during the shot, it will not help the editor.

This headroom is too little.

It might look as if the woman is bobbing up and down.

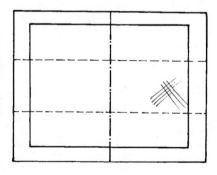

A mask made of see-through plastic marked with headrooms, safe areas and centre lines can be placed over the screen of the field monitor.

Keep spurious objects out of the shot

Reasons

A spurious object is anything, however small or large, that distracts the viewer. It draws the attention away from the subject of the shot to itself.

Spurious objects in the foreground, for example, a dog walking unexpectedly across the shot, are the worst cases, and are very obvious. Background spurious objects are harder to recognise, but can cause equal problems in later stages of production.

There are many sorts of spurious objects, ranging from badly framed backgrounds, to 'passers-by' waving to camera. Colour can often become a spurious object. For example, a small amount of foreground colour in an out of focus background will draw attention to itself by distracting the viewer away from the subject.

Equally spurious is interviewing a subject in front of a computer screen which itself contains activity unrelated to what is being discussed. Invariably the viewers will be more curious about the spurious object than they will be about the subject.

Exceptions

The main exception to this practice is when the spurious object is part of the script, as in drama or, in documentary shooting, where to omit it would reduce the value of the shot; or, in news, where it is part of the reality and the instantaneous value of the shot.

Another exception is when the spurious object is shot in such a way as to be completely out of focus and is hence unrecognisable.

The main guideline is not to have a spurious object of any kind in the shot, unless it is part of the story.

The background frame becomes a spurious object.

A badly positioned subject.

The activity on the computer screen becomes as important as the subject.

When framing more than two subjects, frame in depth

Reasons
The framing of shots falls into a well-defined pattern. When more than two persons are in the frame, with some shots it becomes clear that they will not fit into the frame easily. Screen space becomes a priority.

Solutions
As the shot cannot be made wider, then the subjects must be arranged in depth, from front to back. Even then, care must be taken with the edges of the frame. If a subject cuts the edge of the frame in the foreground or in the middleground it will be noticeable. In the background less so. It is important to keep even middleground action away from the 10% loss area which will be experienced around the edge of the frame.

Exceptions
The main exception to this practice is in shooting LS and wider containing a group of many people. Another exception is where the shot is subjective, and the subjects may be having a dialogue with the camera. Exceptions mostly depend upon whether or not the individual subjects are to be recognised as individuals. If they are, the composition takes on immense importance. If the people are not to be recognised, then the composition is relative only to the working practice.

Sometimes a mixture of composing in depth and formal presentation can be had in both objective and subjective shots. A study of the history of painting is a useful source for methods of achieving this.

With three or more subjects, screen space becomes a priority.

By using the depth of the screen, subjects have more space for action and they seem more natural.

Even with the same framing the number of subjects within it may be further increased.

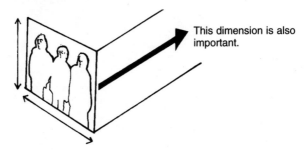

This dimension is also important.

In documentary work, each shot often has a corresponding re-action shot

Nearly all action is a reaction to something else. It is rare in documentary shooting for an action by a subject to be a completely isolated event. Unlike science, the reaction need not be equal and opposite, but it will be corresponding to the action.

Reason
Though the practice is relatively easy to understand with people, it is also true with animals and can be true with inanimate objects. It is so because the audience want it to be so. It is natural curiosity and part of the anthropology of mankind. When man, the hunter, saw or heard a movement of the grass, the reaction was: stay still, look, listen, wait. It would be one of two things, food or danger. Even though human responses have become more camouflaged today, people still respond in a similar way.

Solutions
Observe the subject and shoot each shot keeping in mind the reaction to the shot.

Example
If a man, walking down the street, suddenly looks up, he is doing so for a reason, even if he looks up without knowing. His attention is attracted in the same way as that of 'man the hunter'. Consequently, two shots are required, one of the man walking down the street, and one of that thing or activity which attracted his attention. The action is the man looking, the reaction is that which caused it. These two shots are interchangeable in the next stage of production; the first can come second and the second, the reaction, can come first.

Exceptions
The audience almost know what they want to see before they see it. Making use of this characteristic is common in story telling and has many possibilities in drama. By not showing the reaction to an action, information can be suspended. It may even be denied completely or only revealed later, which is itself a typical device in suspense movies.

The action – the man is walking down the street – he looks up.

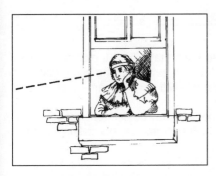

The re-action – this is what he is looking at.

Often the action and re-action are interchangeable. This shot could be the action.

But this shot could also be the action and the man the re-action.

Shoot matched shots rather than unmatched shots

Reason

A matched shot, also known as a reverse angle shot, is a shot taken from the opposite point of view to the preceding one. This working practice refers mainly to shooting dialogue between two people only. The fundamental reason is to present shots to the editor which when edited, centre the audience's attention on the action or dialogue, without any variations in background or framing.

A matched shot must be similar, if not the same, as its opposite shot in three ways:

1. It should have the same camera angle.
2. It should have the the same distance from the subject.
3. It should have the same lens angle.

Assuming two people are talking to each other, then the same camera angle will give the same view of each of the subjects. The same distance from the subjects with the same lens angle will give the same framing and the same depth of field in both the shots.

Even though the backgrounds in one shot may be different from those of the other, providing the depth of field is the same, then the definition of the backgrounds will be similar.

Exceptions

An exception is when there is physically not enough space to shoot a matching shot. In this case it would be wiser, in the case of an interview, either to choose somewhere larger or to change the method of the interview to fit the camera and framing available.

It is also possible to have a reverse angle shot which is not matching, but this generally refers to framing in drama, rather than in interviews.

A matched shot has three requirements.

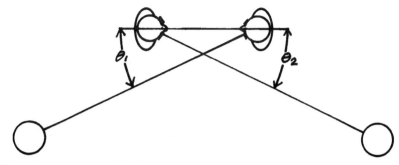

The same camera angle, $\theta_1 = \theta_2$.

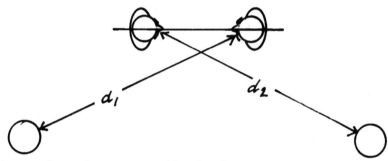

The same distance from camera to subject, $d_1 = d_2$.

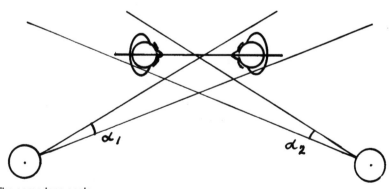

The same lens angle, $\alpha_1 = \alpha_2$

Providing the lens aperture is similar, the lens depth of field will also be similar, and then the shots will 'match'.

In a three person dialogue never shoot matching a two shot

Reason
The reason lies in the needs of post-production. When, within a three person dialogue, a two shot is edited to a two shot, the subject in the centre position will appear to move from one side of the screen to the other.

Example
Three people are talking, persons A, B and C. Person B is in the middle and an attempt at matching is made using the 'two shot'. Obviously, person B will be on both shots. In the first shot, B is on the left-hand side of the screen and, in the second shot, B will have moved to the right-hand side of the screen. Clearly these two shots would jump if the editor tried to cut them together.

Solutions
It follows that, in a three person group, there is no such thing as a matching 'two shot'. Consequently, shoot so that a 'two shot' of say persons B and C can be followed by a shot of person A alone, or the opposite way around.

Another method is to use a complex shot. This can be done by a pan from a two shot to another two shot, PROVIDING there is good enough motivation to make the pan.

Exceptions
When shooting four people in a group, then the 'two shot' will match.

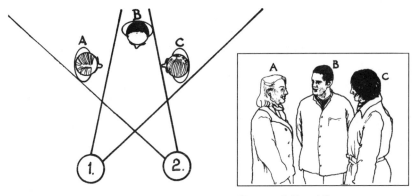

Persons A, B and C

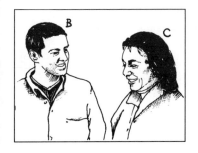

Two shot from position 1

Two shot from position 2

These two shots, even though they are matching, will not edit.

These two shots will edit but care must be taken when shooting person A as an MCU that the frame does not contain the edges of person B.

When shooting head shots of a subject, the more full face the shot is, the better

Reason

The more the camera angle approaches full face, the more facial expression is gained. An important element of the facial expression is centred on the eyes, and consequently, the more the two eyes are in frame, the more convincing the shot is to the audience, because the eyeline is closer to theirs.

Obviously, if the camera angle is actually on the eyeline, then the shot changes from being an objective shot to a subjective shot.

Solutions

In the case of the objective shot, the aim would be to have a camera angle close enough to the eyeline of the subject to have the most convincing facial expression, but not so close that it appears that the subject is talking direct to the camera.

Example

With two subjects facing each other, the full face practice applies even more. However, the closer the camera angle approaches the eyeline, the more likely the shot is to be contaminated by a spurious foreground. Also, the closer the two subjects are to each other, the less likely the cameraman is to obtain a 'clean' simple shot of one of the subjects. The further they stand apart, the easier the simple shot becomes, but the more difficult the well framed over shoulder shot becomes.

With a single subject there can be no over shoulder shot, and consequently, the camera angle can be very small.

Exceptions

The exception to this practice is in a shot which needs to restrict visual information. Then the shot becomes more of a profile.

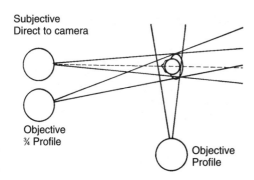

Subjective
Direct to camera

Objective
¾ Profile

Objective
Profile

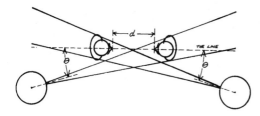

Over shoulder   Over shoulder

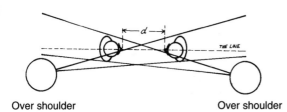

To obtain a 'clean' shot the camera angle (θ) must be increased.

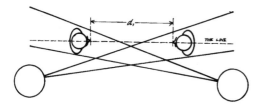

OR the distance between the subjects d_1 must be increased.

165

When shooting the rise in two separate shots, allow sufficient double action

The rise is the name given to a subject action which rises from one level to another. Thus the action of a seated subject, who then stands, is called a rise.

The rise can be shot in one complex shot, or two simple shots. This working practice refers to the rise being shot with two simple shots.

Reason

Overlapping action must be included on both shots to allow the editor to cut action at an exact frame on both shots when the continuity is identical. The rise is often considered slightly more difficult because, in the case of standing from a sitting position, the body does not move only in one direction but in three.

Example

A subject is to rise, sitting to standing. Two simple shots are called for: one, an MS from the front of the subject; and the second, an LS, shot at 90 degrees from the first. In the first shot, the head will come forward before the knees straighten, and then the body rises so that the head exits the frame and the camera finishes shooting the waist. In the second shot, the action is from the beginning of the movement to the end of the complete action.

The editor will try to cut the shot so that the eyes of the subject never leave the first shot.

The sequence is a little easier the other way around, i.e. from LS into MS, but care must be taken when shooting to position the rise on the LS so that the head is approximately in the same position within the screen as in the MS.

Exceptions

When shooting for a continuity (action) edit, there are no exceptions to the overlapping action requirement. Obviously this is not so when shooting the rise in one complex shot.

166

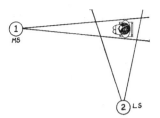

SHOT 1 MS

MS (direct to camera) subject seated.

The head comes forward and consequently appears larger.

The subject comes even closer and lens distortion becomes possible. The subject begins to rise and the eyes reach the upper frame.

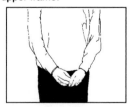

The head has left the screen and the subject is now fully standing.

SHOT 2 LS

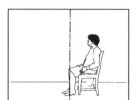

LS (profile) subject seated and set for a rise to the centre screen.

The subject leans forward (screen left) and the head takes the position above the instep of the foot.

The subject begins the rise as the head continues to move screen left and also upwards.

The rise completed, where the head resumes its balanced position above the instep.

167

When shooting a close-up of an action, as a cut-away, shoot a slightly slower version

Reason
An action on a wide shot covers a small amount of screen. When the same action is seen in close-up, the real time of the action remains constant, but the action travels further.

It appears that action in close-up shots takes less time to complete than the same action in a wide shot.

Example
A woman sitting at a desk hears the telephone ring; she picks it up and answers it. Say the scene calls for two shots. Shot 1 is the woman reaching down for the telephone, picking it up and answering. Shot 2 is a close shot of the telephone being picked up and will be edited into shot 1. In shot 1, MCU or wider, the hand will travel up to half way across the screen before the editor will cut out of it. In shot 2, the close-up, the hand, whilst still travelling in the same direction, will cover almost the area of the screen in less time. Even though the action is the same real time in both shots, the action when on close-up will seem faster because the shot is concentrated on one small area.

Solution
Shoot a version of the hand picking up the telephone slightly slower than the real action.

Exceptions
When shooting live, or with two synchronised cameras.

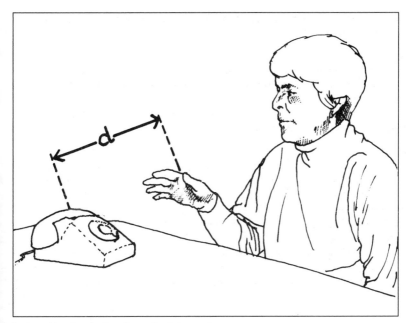

In the wide shot the hand travels distance d.

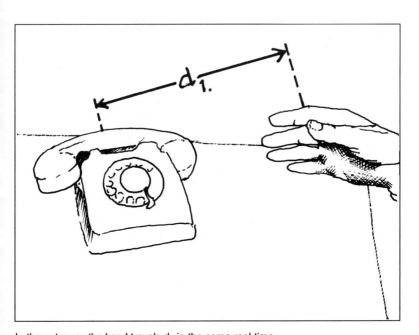

In the cut-away the hand travels d_1 in the same real time.

Never let a zoom be seen

A zoom is an infinite set of fixed focal length lenses. The mechanism of moving from one focal length lens to another is called zooming.

Reason

A zoom is a mechanical method of lens selection. As such, it is an obvious visual part of the mechanism which becomes an obtrusive movement because it is impossible in normal vision. The eyes do not zoom. The relationship of the background to the foreground in normal vision is based on a set of visual clues which have a relationship to each other and make for balance and understanding for the audience. If this relationship is broken or disturbed, as with the action of a zoom, then the understanding and realism is lost.

Solution

This practice does not mean that a zoom should not be used, only that it must not be seen to be used. Consequently, a zoom should never be used on its own. The mechanical action should be covered or camouflaged with a more realistic camera movement to draw the attention of the audience away from the unrealistic movement. As the lens movement is part of the complex shot, it follows that another component of the complex shot can act as the camouflaging agent. Thus a pan will help to cover a zoom, as will a tilt. Also, the zoom can be well camouflaged within a developing shot, for example, as with a track and zoom.

Exceptions

There are three exceptions which make a zoom permissible.

1. In hot news, where there may be no alternative to the zoom, because of either time or accessibility.
2. When using the 'creeping zoom' – a zoom which is so slow in its change that the movement cannot easily be noticed by the audience.
3. When the background is virtually neutral so that there is no noticeable change between foreground and background, and hence the zoom may resemble a track.

Never track out without motivation

Reason

A track in represents the natural human trait of wanting to get closer in order to observe more clearly. A track out, however, represents a person walking away and also backwards as a form of formal ending.

Whilst the track in is usual, a track out is unusual.

Example

The track out is often used as the visual translation of the end of a formal meeting with the King or Emperor. The flunkey or servant, never being allowed to turn his back on the King, must walk backwards away from his presence. In adapting this meaning to shooting, the track out represents the formal end of a scene, or the end of a part of the story, or the end of the story itself. Because of what the movement represents, it needs some specific motivation to make it worthwhile.

Solution

The most common motivation in a drama for the track out is from the action of the subject. In some way the camera is forced back by an action within the scene. For example, in the last shot, as 'the only train to escape the Indian Salinman Mutiny steams, with a final triumphal whistle, home to the safety of Platform 4 at Calcutta Railway Station', it would be the action of the train coming forward into the shot which would motivate the track out to begin.

The motivation can be strengthened by appropriate sound, but it should not be represented only by a piece of music.

Exceptions

There are as many exceptions to this practice as there are story endings.

When shooting machinery, observe the 'line'

Reason
Objects such as people have a line. The line, when used to clarify our viewing position of machinery, has the same directional problems as any other subject, animate or inanimate. This is as true for horizontal and vertical movement, as it is for rotational movement.

Example
A wheel rotating in a clockwise direction as viewed from one side of the line will appear to rotate in an anticlockwise direction from the other side of the line. Obviously, the wheel has not changed its rotational direction. The wheel can only go in one direction, but if two shots, one from each side of the line were edited together, it would appear to do so.

Solution
Shoot from one side of the line only.

Exceptions
Only if the speed of the machinery is so fast that a change of direction might not be seen by the audience. Whilst this might be true with rotating machinery, it is unlikely with reciprocating machinery.

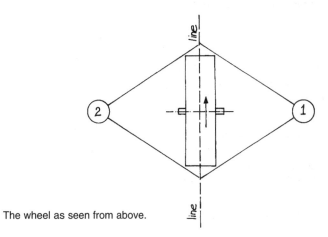

The wheel as seen from above.

Shot 2

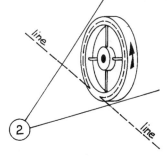

Shot 1

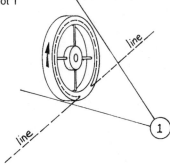

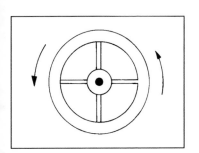

The wheel appears to turn anticlockwise

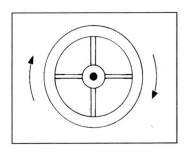

The wheel appears to turn clockwise.

Cross the line with care

Reason

Any subject shot from both sides of the line will result in a directional change of some sort. Either this directional change can be used within the story, or it must be camouflaged by some other movement or shot.

There are only a limited number of ways to effectively cross the line.

Solution

Method 1: Be seen to cross the line. This would need a developing shot of the subject, beginning on one side of the line and, in vision, crossing the line and finishing on the opposite side. As the audience has seen it happen, it is accepted because the eye is capable of appreciating what is happening. However, if there is no motivation for the movement of the camera in the developing shot, then another method should be used.

Method 2: Shoot an 'in between' shot, on the line. This means shooting the sequence from one side to the other in a number of simple shots where one of those shots is taken from on the line. In this way the audience is led from one side to the other by a 'sampling' of positions.

Method 3: Shoot a 'cut-away'. A shot of another subject related to the main subject, or even part of it, draws the audience's attention away from the line to this new subject, after which the attention can be brought back to the opposite side of the line. This method relies on there being a time interval between seeing one side of the line and returning to the opposite side.

Exception

An exception when a change of direction is required by nature of the activity or of the story.

WAYS OF CROSSING THE LINE

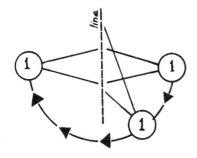

Method 1
Be seen crossing the line with one continuous shot.

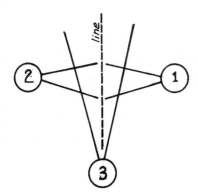

Method 2
Shoot an in-between shot on the line.

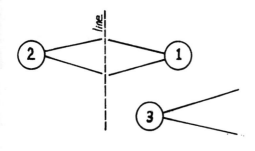

Method 3
Shoot a 'cut-away' of another, but related subject.

175

Clear the screen, the action or the shot, before the shot ends

Reason
This practice, whilst applying mainly to documentary shooting, also applies to drama work. The main reason for it is the need, during editing of the shots, for a time interval between one shot with its activity and a following shot with another activity. This time interval allows the editor greater possibilities in the final selection of the editing point.

Example – Clear the screen
A woman, shot LS, is walking across the screen, left to right. Providing the woman is allowed to exit the screen completely, the next shot can have the woman walking right to left, because there is a suggested time interval during which the woman can have changed direction. This time interval is the combined lengths on both shots which do not contain the woman, in this case the end of one shot and the beginning of another.

Example – Clear the action
The subject is to use the telephone. Two shots are called for, one an MCU of the subject looking down at the telephone; and the second shot is the hand of the subject punching the numbers. The action of punching up to twelve numbers will be followed with either the hand remaining on shot, or the hand exiting shot. Even if the hand remains on shot, the number of editing possibilities is increased because the action, the punching of the buttons, has been cleared or completed.

Example – Clear the shot
At the end of a pan, a man has walked to a door. He opens the door, passes through and closes it behind him. The shot should continue until the door has been closed, with the framing the same as the end framing of the pan.

Exceptions
There are no exceptions to this practice.

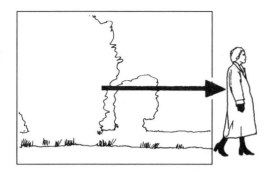

Let the subject clear the screen completely.

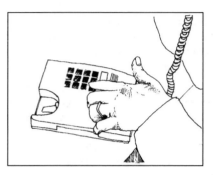

Finish the action.

At the end of the pan …

… let the door close, wait, then end the shot.

In documentary shooting, observe but never intrude

Reason
When taking a shot in a public area, a camera, crew and equipment are obtrusive. The attention of the public, because of natural curiosity, is inevitably drawn to anything out of the ordinary. As soon as a crew sets up, often the activity which they came to shoot can change because of their very presence. In Western countries the situations are almost predictable. But this is not the case in some countries where a crew might be breaking the law simply by being there, much less having a camera.

A cameraman should never be obtrusive. Observe but never interfere.

Example
A shot must be taken of a subject who will either disappear or stop the shot when the subject realises it is being taken. For example, a soldier guarding a highly sensitive building. The soldier will interfere with or, in some countries, arrest the crew, if he has reason to think that security is being compromised.

Solution
Position the crew so that they are camouflaging the camera from the view of the subject. The crew should point and obviously discuss something which is opposite to that of the subject. The lens should be pointing through a small, but purposely left, gap between the crew, ideally around waist height. The subject, because of natural curiosity, will be looking where the crew is looking and should not notice the lens.

For simple situations, use a hide or screen. Try positioning on the opposite side of a road (lens permitting) or behind a car or van. The use of existing local 'cover' is better than a strange or unusual one.

Exceptions
Exceptions are news gathering, interviewing, small interiors and any situation that needs extra lighting. In these situations a camera and crew are very obtrusive.

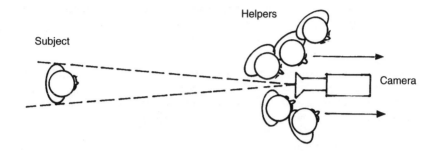

The crew or helpers block the camera from the view of the subject and look and gesture (if required) in a direction opposite to the camera.

Beware continuity traps

A continuity trap is an object or activity within a shot which contains a change caused by the passage of time. For example a clock.

Reason

Any sequence made up of a number of shots containing a continuity trap will show those changes when the sequence is edited together. Because the changes occur shot by shot, then the shots with their time changes become a part of the sequence and may be noticed by the audience.

Continuity traps should either be used correctly or eliminated from the shot.

Examples

A subject is smoking a cigarette. Each time a shot is made the length of the cigarette will change.

A clock, shown in shot, will indicate one time. The same clock shown in another shot will show a different time.

Continuity traps are very common and the results, if not noticed and overcome, can result in significant problems in the editing of shots. Particular care should be taken with sun shadows, plants that respond quickly to time or the sun, some background sounds etc.

Solution

Either remove the trap, change the camera angle so the trap is never in shot or alter the trap so that it can be contained in the shot. For example, if a clock must be in shot because of the story, then the clock should be stopped, thus giving the same time on each shot.

Normally the problems of continuity traps are overcome by a specially appointed person, but in small crews without continuity support, it is the cameraman who must be aware of them.

180

Exceptions
The only exception to this practice is when the time change, or even the continuity trap, is part of the story.

When shooting the pan, position your body correctly

The pan has three parts, the start frame, the panning head movement and the end frame. The viewer should see only the movement of the subject in the pan, never the pan itself. Consequently the cameraman must use his own body together with the pan and tilt head to achieve the best result. To obtain maximum smoothness in the pan and perfect stability in the start and end frames, the cameraman must position his body to suit the END frame rather than the start frame.

Reasons

There are four reasons for this practice.

- It is smoother to twist the waist than it is the neck.
- Turning INTO balance and stability is smoother and more controllable than turning away from it.
- Within the time span of a pan, the cameraman is in balance for a longer period of time than he would be out of it.
- It eliminates 'drift' on the end frame.

It follows that the cameraman should pan into a normal position rather than panning away from it.

Example

Say a pan is required that follows a subject over a distance requiring 180 degrees of movement. Proceed as follows.

1. Set up the shot for the end frame. Take a wide, but comfortable, balanced foot position facing the end frame.
2. Without moving the feet, twist the waist and bring the camera back to the start frame.
3. As the pan begins, the camera and the cameraman's body, locked together, immediately begin to gain fluidity. At the end frame the body, and hence the camera, are in a controllable position.

Exceptions

The exceptions to this practice are when using a geared pan and tilt head operated by a rotating handle, when using a crane or similar camera mounting, or when the pan is completing only a small radial movement.

SHOOTING THE PAN

Set up the shot for the end frame.

Without moving the feet twist the waist to bring the camera to the start frame. As the pan begins ...

let the waist revolve ...

in a fluid movement ...

to finish in a controlled body position at the end frame.

183

Never track using more than a 40 degree lens angle

Lens angle means the angle of view of the lens. There is a mathematical relationship between:

- the image width on the photo surface, tube or chip;
- the focal length (the distance the lens is from the photo surface, measured in mm); and
- the angle of view of the lens.

The lens is either quoted in mm (meaning focal length) or by degrees (meaning lens angle). Film cameramen traditionally referred to their lens by focal length. TV cameramen used lens angle. Estimating for shots on-site, for studio or floor plans is usually in terms of lens angle.

When shooting tracks some adverse effects occur with some lens settings.

Reason

A track carried out with a lens angle of over 40 degrees will curve what should be vertical lines. In a simple shot, where there is no movement of the camera, this bending of a vertical is always noticeable. But when the shot is a complex or developing one, i.e. when the camera is moving, then the amount of curvature becomes very obvious.

Solution

Keep below 40 degrees of lens angle, or use a more superior lens.

LENS ANGLE/FOCAL LENGTH LOOK-UP TABLE

	FORMAT	
	½" VIDEO	⅔" VIDEO
Image width		
Inches	0.5	0.567
mm	12.7	16.93
	1.33:1	1.33:1
Lens focal length (mm)		
400	1.8	2.4
250	2.9	3.9
200	3.6	4.8
150	4.8	6.5
135	5.4	7.2
100	7.3	9.7
85	8.5	11
75	10	13
50	14	19
40	18	24
35	21	27
30	24	32
27	26	35
25	29	37
20	35	46
17	41	53
14.5	47	61
10	65	80
Lens angle (°)		
1	728	970
1.5	485	647
2	364	485
3	242	323
4	182	242
5	145	194
7	104	138
10	73	97
15	48	64
20	36	48
25	29	38
30	24	32
40	17	23
50	14	18
60	11	15
80	8	10
100	5	7

Never track in using less than a 20 degree lens angle

Reason
There are two reasons for this practice.

1. The difficulty in keeping the subject in focus during the track.
2. The smallest defect in the track mechanism would be magnified on the screen.

Example – focus problems
A track is called for, down a corridor, following a subject walking from A to B. Two examples are shown. In the first, a narrow angle lens (less than 20 degrees) is shown. The depth of field would be so small that any variation in the distance between A and C would result in the subject being out of focus. This variation could be in the length of the subject's footsteps, speed of walk, or speed of the track, or any combination of them. Holding focus would be very difficult.

Solution
In the second version the lens angle has been increased to between 30 and 40 degrees. The distance between A and C is much shorter, so that the physical area needed to shoot the track is much smaller (an important factor if the interior is being used by others); but, additionally, the depth of field is much greater. Consequently, the subject has a greater chance of being held in focus.

Example – track defects
All tracks have defects, however small they may be, for example, a joint between the pipes. This small jerk as the wheels go over it transmits itself to the camera as a vibration. Seen on a small screen it is noticeable. Seen on a large screen it looks like a bumpy road.

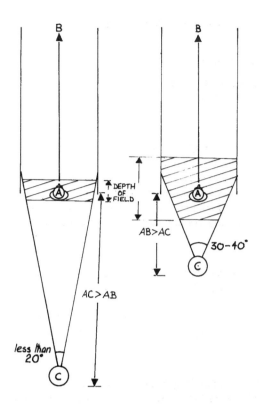

Depth of field
The near and far distances within which a subject is in focus.

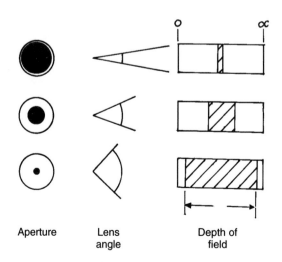

Aperture Lens angle Depth of field

187

Solution
The solution lies in reducing the distance from A to C, from camera to subject. Imagine C as being the centre of a circle with A on its circumference. A is joined to C as the radius. Somewhere along the line A to C, closer to C, is another point X. If A were to move around the circumference for a large distance, it would only move X a small distance. Rather like waving a flag, a small distance moved at the wrist makes for a bigger distance moved by the top of the flag.

So, reducing the distance from camera to subject gives a wider lens angle, which tends not to show track discrepancies.

Exceptions
In some dramatic shots, like a disaster earth tremor sequence, the foreground and background will sometimes move together. Here the narrow angle is very useful. Holding foreground subjects in focus still remains a problem.

In a dramatic sequence the disadvantage of using the wide angle is that the tracks are laid within the lens view. Consequently, the subject must step within them or around them. This is not the case with the narrow angle track.

For natural perspective on a wide shot, keep the camera horizontal
Wide shot refers to a lens angle over 40 degrees.

Reason
Any wide angle lens will distort to a certain extent. If the shot is taken with the camera horizontal, that is, without tilt, the distortion should be unnoticeable. However, when the camera is in the tilt position, either low angle pointing up, or high angle pointing down, then perspective distortion takes place.

The closer the camera is to the subject when using a tilt, the more the distortion takes effect until the distortion becomes obtrusive.

Example
A man stands at the foot of a tall factory chimney. A subjective shot is required showing what he sees, looking up. Natural perspective will indicate that the top of the chimney is smaller than the bottom. The line of the edges of the building seem to lean in, or parallel lines would seem to converge.

If this shot were taken with a lens of over 40 degrees, then this convergence is emphasised and distorted to such an extent that, to be acceptable to the audience, the man would need to be standing with his chin against the tower looking up.

Solution
When shooting with a wide angle take care not to stray too far from the horizontal camera position. If a tilted shot is required, then a narrower angle should be used.

The practice is also true in the reverse situation, looking down.

Exceptions
The exception is shots which must emphasise height, weight or unbalance. These can be obtained using both a tilt and very wide lens angles. Another exception might be in a subjective shot representing a subject suffering from a phobia; for example, vertigo.